Caring for a cat with hyperthyroidism

by Dr Sarah Caney

Published by Vet Professionals Ltd

Copyright © Vet Professionals Ltd 2013

www.vetprofessionals.com

ISBN 978-1-908583-03-1

About Cat Professional

Cat Professional is a subdivision of Vet Professionals Ltd. Cat Professional was founded in 2007 by Dr Sarah Caney with the aims of providing cat owners and veterinary professionals with the highest quality information, advice, training and consultancy services.

Publications

Cat Professional is a leading provider of high quality publications on caring for cats with a variety of medical conditions. Written by international experts in their field, each book is written to be understood by cat owners and veterinary professionals. The books are available to buy through the website www.catprofessional.com as eBooks where they can be downloaded and read instantly. Alternatively they can be purchased as a softback via the website and good bookstores.

'Caring for a cat with hyperthyroidism' was first published in 2009, this updated edition was published in April 2013. Other books in the Cat Professional series include:

- 'Caring for a blind cat' by Natasha Mitchell
- 'Caring for a cat with lower urinary tract disease' by Dr Sarah Caney and Professor Danièlle Gunn-Moore
- 'Caring for a cat with chronic kidney disease' by Dr Sarah Caney
- 'Caring for an overweight cat' by Andrea Harvey and Samantha Taylor

A variety of free-to-download articles also feature on the Cat Professional website.

Advice, Training and Consultancy

Cat Professional is dedicated to improving the standards of cat care and in this capacity is a provider of Continuing Professional Development to veterinarians, veterinary nurses and other professionals working with cats around the world.

Cat Professional also works closely with leading providers of cat products and foods providing training programmes, assisting with product literature and advising on product design and marketing.

Free-to-download articles articles and technical documents of interest to cat owners and veterinary professionals are available on the website.

Specialist feline medicine advice is available to veterinary professionals and cat owners world-wide. Details are available on the website.

About the author

Sarah Caney (pictured right) is an internationally recognised veterinary specialist in feline medicine who has worked as a feline-only vet since 1994. She trained as a specialist at the University of Bristol, England and is one of only fourteen recognised specialists in feline medicine working within the UK. Sarah has written many articles for veterinarians and cat owners and works very closely with the UK cat charity, the Feline Advisory Bureau, FAB (www.fabcats.org). Sarah has written two other books published by Cat Professional: 'Caring for a cat with chronic kidney disease and 'Caring for a cat with lower urinary tract disease' (the latter co-authored with Professor Danièlle Gunn-Moore). As a clinician she enjoys seeing a mixture of first opinion and referral feline patients. She has been invited to lecture on feline medicine at veterinary conferences all over the world.

The cat pictured below right is Hobi, Sarah's very special elderly cat. Sadly Hobi died as a result of various medical problems, including hyperthyroidism, in April 2011.

About this book

This book has been written as both a printed book and interactive electronic book. Words in green are contained in the glossary section at the end of the book.

Dedications and acknowledgements

Thanks go to all of those colleagues, clients and friends for their advice on what should be included and, of course, to the cats pictured for all looking so gorgeous!

The pictures included in this book are the copyright of the author with the exception of:

- 'Shortcake', the hypothyroid kitten shown on page 52, included with the kind permission of Professor Tim Gruffydd-Jones.
- The pictures of Anna shown on page 66, included with the kind permission of her owner
- Pictures of the Wilkinson cats shown on pages 67-69 included with the kind permission of their owner Kathy and professional cat photographer Robert Fox (www.photopaws.co.uk).
- The picture of Lucy, shown on page 70, taken by her owner Lynda

CONTENTS

Hyperthyroidism is considered to be a relatively 'new' illness since it was first diagnosed in 1979 in the United States. Since this time, the frequency of this diagnosis has increased with one recent study suggesting that 12% of the UK cat population over the age of nine years are diagnosed with this condition each year. Similar results have been reported in Australia, Germany, Japan and the United States. A recent publication reported that the frequency of hyperthyroidism in US cats is increasing and many UK vets also feel that this illness is becoming more common. This might be because of increased awareness of the disease (and hence it is being tested for more often) but could also be a result of the increasing life-length of many cats. Since we still do not fully understand the cause of hyperthyroidism, it is also possible that the disease is becoming more common for other reasons. Worldwide, hyperthyroidism is believed to be the most common hormonal disease in cats with diabetes mellitus ('sugar diabetes') a close second. The frequency of hyperthyroidism varies quite markedly according to where the cat lives – for example it is a common diagnosis in the US and UK but rarely diagnosed in Greece and Scandinavian countries.

This guide has been written to provide care providers with the information they need to understand this complex condition and provide the best care for their cat. The author regularly lectures on this subject and the contents of this book reflect what she teaches to veterinary students, veterinary nurses, technicians and qualified veterinarians around the world.

Receiving the news: coping with the emotional side of receiving a diagnosis of hyperthyroidism

Being told that your cat has hyperthyroidism may have caused you some concern. Hyperthyroidism is a complicated condition to understand. This section will aim to reassure you as well as prepare you for what is to come.

What is wrong with my cat?

Hyperthyroidism is the veterinary term used to describe an illness resulting from having excessively high blood levels of thyroid hormones. All cats have a thyroid gland composed of two portions (referred to as thyroid 'lobes') in their neck. The thyroid hormones are required in healthy cats for many functions including normal growth and development and maintenance of a normal metabolic rate. Excessive blood levels of thyroid hormones (such as is the case with hyperthyroidism) are damaging to the body and ultimately this is a fatal illness if not treated.

Section 2 covers the scientific aspects of this condition in much greater detail – you can read about what we know about the causes of this condition, how veterinarians diagnose hyperthyroidism and how it can best be treated. The good news is that this is considered to be a treatable condition – many cats can be cured of their clinical signs with appropriate treatment.

Could I have prevented this from happening – was it my fault?

Many people will immediately panic, thinking that they could have done more to prevent an illness from developing or that, if only they had taken their cat to the veterinarian sooner, things might be different. Although it is impossible to generalise or comment specifically on an individual cat's circumstances, it is worth remembering that:

- Hyperthyroidism is not caused by anything that you as an owner or care provider have done
- Although this is a condition which will get progressively worse with time, in most situations a short delay is unlikely to have changed your cat's chance of recovery.

What is the treatment for this disease?

There are four main treatment options for hyperthyroid cats:

- Medical treatment: prescribing antithyroid drugs which block production of thyroid hormones
- Nutritional management: feeding an iodine-restricted food which limits the production of thyroid hormones
- Surgical treatment: removal of the diseased thyroid tissue
- Radioiodine treatment: also referred to as radioactive iodine therapy, this is a form of radiotherapy that is able to treat abnormal thyroid tissue.

Some hyperthyroid cats need additional medication for complications associated with their hyperthyroidism. For example, high blood pressure (systemic hypertension) is seen in a significant proportion of hyperthyroid cats and requires specific treatment.

Since hyperthyroidism is a condition which is common in older cats, it is not unusual for them to have more than one medical problem. Other common illnesses in older cats include a decline in kidney function (chronic kidney disease) and diabetes mellitus ('sugar diabetes'). If present, these conditions also require treatment.

All of the treatments are discussed in more detail in Section 2.

Is my cat in pain?

Hyperthyroidism is not believed to be a painful condition although some of the symptoms of illness can be distressing to a cat. For example, breathlessness, palpitations, irritability and anxiety can be seen with this condition.

Is it fair to put my cat on medication – am I being cruel to treat it?

Hyperthyroidism is considered to be a very treatable condition and it is possible to cure the illness in many cases. Not all cats require long-term medication, as this depends on which of the treatments is prescribed and whether the cat has other illnesses requiring therapy.

In many hyperthyroid cats, however, successful treatment involves long-term courses of medication. If your cat has been prescribed medication and you are concerned about how you may be able to give this to your cat, then it may be helpful to hear that:

- Some cats are surprisingly easy to medicate

- Some cats will eat treatments reliably in their food

- In some countries, transdermal treatments are available for hyperthyroidism. These come as a skin cream which is usually applied to the inside of the cat's ear (a hairless area). The medication is absorbed through the skin and into the blood stream. Transdermal treatments are discussed in more detail on page 33

- For those cats on multiple medications empty gelatine capsules obtained from a veterinarian or pharmacist can be very helpful. Several medicines can be put into one empty gelatine capsule reducing medication into one easy dosage

- Advice on how to administer pills to a cat is contained on pages 36-40 and a link to a video showing how to give a pill to a cat is listed in the 'Useful websites' section.

It may take some time for you, and your cat, to get used to the treatment your veterinarian has suggested but as long as your cat

Left: Some cats are very easy to medicate with pills or capsules.

is happy and coping, it is worthwhile persevering. Don't forget to discuss how treatment is going with your veterinarian – if you are having problems, they may well have solutions or suggestions for you.

Also, remember that we are talking about *your* cat – no one knows your cat better than you and if you feel that the treatment suggested is not right, for whatever reason, then your veterinarian should respect this.

I'm not sure I can cope with treating my cat – help!

Learning of a diagnosis of hyperthyroidism may have come as a shock and will take some time to get used to. Once you have had a chance to think things through, chat with friends/family and your veterinarian, hopefully everything will seem clearer and less daunting.

You can only do your best when it comes to caring for your cat and it is not always possible to do everything you want. For example if you have severe arthritis and are unable to give your cat a pill this may affect the level of treatment you can provide. Likewise, if your cat is completely intolerant to the thought of being medicated, this may prevent you from giving some treatments to it. In many situations, there are other options available – for example trying to hide medications in food or considering treatments which do not involve daily medications such as feeding an iodine-restricted food, performing surgery or radioiodine. In any case, your veterinarian should be able to talk you through the options and, together, you should be able to make a plan that you both feel comfortable with. The treatments for hyperthyroidism are discussed in more detail in Section 2.

> **Hyperthyroidism is a treatable condition – many cats can be cured with appropriate therapy**

Is hyperthyroidism life-threatening?

If left untreated, hyperthyroidism will eventually result in death as this illness has serious consequences on internal organs such as the heart. With appropriate treatment it is considered to be an illness which can be controlled and often cured.

This is discussed in more detail in Section 2.

What is hyperthyroidism?

Hyperthyroidism is the medical term for a situation where there are excessive blood levels of thyroid hormones. Some clinicians call this condition thyrotoxicosis. Thyroid hormones are produced by the thyroid gland. There are two thyroid hormones – T3 (triiodothyronine) and T4 (thyroxine).

What effect do thyroid hormones have on the body?

Thyroid hormones act on most body cells and in general their effects are to:

- increase the metabolic rate
- increase the heart rate (number of heart beats per minute) and the force of each heart beat
- increase blood pressure
- increase gastrointestinal (bowel) movement which can cause diarrhoea and/or vomiting
- increase activity levels – affected cats can be very restless and hyperactive
- reduce bodyweight (i.e. cause weight loss)
- reduce the amount of time the cat spends asleep
- aid in control of body temperature (thermoregulation).

What is the thyroid gland and what does a healthy thyroid gland do?

The thyroid gland is normally located in the cat's neck, just below the larynx (voice box). The thyroid gland is made up of two lobes – one on each side of the neck. Some cats also have 'ectopic' (sometimes clinicians use the term 'accessory') thyroid tissue. Ectopic is the medical term for tissue at an unusual location. Ectopic thyroid tissue can be found under the tongue, in the neck and, most commonly, in the chest cavity.

Iodine present in the food is absorbed into the circulation where it is taken to the thyroid gland. Iodine is actively concentrated in the thyroid where it is used to make the thyroid hormones, T3 and T4. Both of these hormones are released into the circulation from where they can act on all of the cells of the body. Thyroid hormones are required to regulate the body's metabolism. Production and release of thyroid hormones is under tight control in healthy cats. The hormone TRH (thyrotropin releasing hormone, produced in a part of the brain called the hypothalamus) stimulates production of TSH (thyrotropin or thyroid stimulating hormone, produced in a part of the brain called the pituitary) which in turn stimulates production and release of the thyroid hormones. Presence of T4 and T3 inhibits production of TRH and TSH so that levels of these thyroid hormones remain within a healthy balance. In hyperthyroid cats, the thyroid gland 'ignores' TSH and works autonomously (under its own control). The end result of this is abnormally high blood levels of thyroid hormones which causes a range of problems, as discussed later.

What causes hyperthyroidism?

There is still much not known about the cause of hyperthyroidism. This is a relatively new illness (first diagnosed in the United States in 1979) which varies in frequency around the world and even within individual countries. These findings have led to theories that genetic, dietary and/or environmental factors might be to blame for the disease. The belief that feline genetics may play a role in the development of hyperthyroidism is supported by the fact that one study showed that Siamese and Himalayan breed cats were ten times *less* likely to suffer from hyperthyroidism than the rest of the cat population.

Several studies have been done to try and identify common environmental factors which may be involved in causing hyperthyroidism. A recent publication looked at brominated flame retardants (PBDEs: commonly used in soft furnishings and electronic equipment) as these substances have been reported to alter thyroid function in other species. Although older cats tended to have higher levels of these substances than younger cats, no significant association was found between hyperthyroidism and levels of PBDEs. Other studies have looked at nutritional factors such as the iodine content of different foods and tried to assess whether this is a factor in development of the disease. 'Risk factors' – factors increasing the chance that a cat will suffer from hyperthyroidism – have been identified in some studies although much of this data is controversial. For example some studies have shown that eating a wet diet (for example canned foods), having an indoor lifestyle and regular use of flea sprays increases the risk of hyperthyroidism. However, some of these factors are probably more associated with increasing life length of the cat (and hence increasing its chances of developing an illness common in older cats) rather than specific causes of hyperthyroidism. At this stage

Siamese cats are believed to be less vulnerable to developing hyperthyroidism than other cats.

no specific cause has been identified and concerns over hyperthyroidism would not be a good reason to change from a wet to a dry catfood for example.

In the majority of cases, estimated to be 98% or more, hyperthyroidism is caused by a benign overgrowth of the thyroid tissue. This is sometimes referred to as a thyroid adenoma or adenomatous hyperplasia. In less than 2% of cases, hyperthyroidism is caused by a malignant growth (cancer) called a thyroid carcinoma or adenocarcinoma. Thyroid carcinomas are much more serious and need very different treatment from 'routine' hyperthyroid cases. Thyroid carcinomas are discussed in more detail on pages 55-56.

In most cats (estimated > 70%), hyperthyroidism is a bilateral condition – in other words, both lobes of the thyroid gland are affected by the disease. In the remainder of cats, the hyperthyroidism only affects one lobe and so is called unilateral. Some of these cases go on to develop bilateral disease at a later stage in their life.

Which cats most commonly suffer from hyperthyroidism?

Hyperthyroidism is most common in older cats – the most common age group being diagnosed are 10 to 13 years. It is unusual to diagnose hyperthyroidism in cats under seven years of age – less than 5% of cases are diagnosed in this age group. However, this condition has been reported in a few very young cats (the youngest being eight months) although this is very rare. Most studies have indicated that male and female cats appear to be affected with an equal frequency.

Can hyperthyroidism be prevented?

Since the cause of hyperthyroidism has not been identified, at the moment there is little that can be done to prevent this condition. Until we understand the cause of this illness there is no prevention programme that can be recommended.

What are the signs of hyperthyroidism?

The clinical signs of hyperthyroidism vary in severity. Clinical signs are most severe in those cats that have been suffering with the

Weight loss is a common clinical sign associated with hyperthyroidism and can be dramatic.

illness for longer and in those that have additional (also referred to as 'concurrent') illnesses. Chronic kidney disease is one of the most common concurrent illnesses and this results in a worsening of many of the clinical signs.

Clinical signs of hyperthyroidism that a care provider may notice commonly include:

- Weight loss
- An increased hunger and often insatiable appetite (referred to as polyphagia)
- Hyperactivity, anxiety/nervousness and restlessness

A small number of hyperthyroid cats are breathless and/or breathe with their mouth open. Many of these cats are suffering from heart disease as a consequence of their hyperthyroidism.

- An increased thirst (polydipsia) and increased amount of urine produced (polyuria)
- Diarrhoea and/or vomiting
- Poor coat and skin condition, for example matted, greasy and generally unkempt
- Vocalising (often yowling) at night, also referred to as night crying.

Less common clinical signs of hyperthyroidism include:

- Laboured breathing, breathlessness and panting (breathing with the mouth open)
- Weakness, depression and lethargy

- Voice changes
- Reduced or variable appetite
- Heat intolerance – seeking out cool places to sleep.

Cats showing depression, lethargy and reduced appetite are often referred to as 'apathetic' hyperthyroid cases. Some of these cats are even overweight rather than thin. Apathetic means that the cat appears indifferent, showing no emotion or animation. Most apathetic hyperthyroid cats are suffering from severe heart abnormalities associated with their hyperthyroidism.

A veterinary clinical examination may find the following additional abnormalities in a hyperthyroid cat:

- An enlarged thyroid gland that can be felt (the technical term for this is 'palpated') by the veterinarian. An enlarged thyroid is referred to as a 'goitre' or thyroid nodule (a nodule is a lump). The goitre is usually palpated in the neck, just below the larynx (voice box), on one or both sides of the trachea (wind pipe). The size of the goitre can vary enormously. In most cases the goitre is not visible by eye and is the size of a garden pea. In rare cases the goitre can be as large as a golf ball. The goitre is usually mobile to a certain degree – in other words it is possible to move it by a few millimetres under the surface of the skin. In most patients, both thyroid lobes are enlarged ('bilateral' thyroid disease). In some cats, more than two areas of enlarged thyroid can be felt due to disease of normal and ectopic thyroid tissue.

In a small number of cats, the enlarged thyroid cannot be felt. This may be for several reasons:

- The cat may be tense and difficult to examine: it is easiest to feel a thyroid nodule (lump) when the cat is relaxed

In most hyperthyroid cats, the goitre can be felt.

- The thyroid is so enlarged and heavy that it has descended, with gravity, into the chest cavity. Sometimes, 'tipping' the cat gently (holding the back legs up while the cat stands with their forelimb paws on the examination table) can allow the goitre to be felt at the bottom of the neck

- Although the thyroid is producing too much hormone, it is not very large and so difficult to feel

- The diseased thyroid tissue is ectopic – in an abnormal location. Most commonly, ectopic thyroid tissue is located in the chest cavity and hence cannot be felt by a veterinarian. Although the exact frequency of ectopic hyperthyroidism is not known, published reports suggest that up to as many as 20% of hyperthyroid cats may have this condition. Many cats with ectopic hyperthyroid tissue also have a palpable goitre.

In the very small number of cats with malignant thyroid carcinomas, a type of cancer, the thyroid may feel stuck to underlying tissues and/or the skin. In some of these cases, the thyroid may feel more like an area of thickening rather than a specific lump. There may also be some enlargement of lymph glands (lymph nodes) in the same area due to spread of the cancer. Occasionally cats will have a goitre but not be suffering from hyperthyroidism. This can be because the lump is not thyroid tissue (for example being an abscess, lymph tissue or parathyroid tissue) or if the thyroid lump is non-functional (not producing thyroid hormones). The medical term for this is 'euthyroid goitre'. Euthyroid means that the blood levels of thyroid hormones are within the normal (reference) range. Some cats with non-functional thyroid lumps later go on to develop hyperthyroidism. Because of this, many clinicians recommend that cats with a euthyroid goitre have a thyroid hormone blood test done every 6-12 months so that those developing hyperthyroidism can be treated promptly.

- Cardiovascular abnormalities – problems relating to the heart and circulation

  - A rapid heart rate – often faster than 220 beats per minute at a veterinary clinic when healthy cats usually have a heart rate less than 180. The medical term for a fast heart rate is tachycardia

  - A heart murmur audible when listening to the chest with a stethoscope

  - Evidence of high blood pressure – for example damage to the eyes such as retinal detachment – can be seen in some hyperthyroid cats

  - Evidence of congestive heart failure – for example breathlessness and crackly lung sounds in cats with pulmonary oedema (fluid on the lungs) and/or a pleural effusion (fluid in the chest cavity). This is a rare complication of hyperthyroidism.

Even if weight loss has not been noticed by an owner or care provider, it's important to check the cat's weight and body condition score (BCS). The BCS is a measure of whether the cat's weight is normal, increased or decreased for their size. Many cats are good at 'hiding' weight loss so it is sometimes only evident when they are placed on the scales.

What is subclinical hyperthyroidism?

It is now believed that prior to developing obvious clinical signs of hyperthyroidism, most hyperthyroid cats pass through a one to three year period of what is referred to as 'subclinical hyperthyroidism'. Subclinical is the term used when a disease does not show any clinical signs – in other words the cat appears to be completely healthy. Cats with subclinical hyperthyroidism have normal blood levels of thyroid hormones (for example the total T4 remains within the reference range) but their levels of thyroid stimulating hormone (TSH) are persistently low.

Subclinical hyperthyroidism has also been reported to occur commonly in people and some of these may suffer from symptoms of hyperthyroidism affecting their quality of life.

Treatment of subclinical hyperthyroidism is not currently recommended in cats but more frequent monitoring is justified in order to ensure prompt diagnosis and treatment of overt hyperthyroidism once this develops. Monitoring recommendations include:

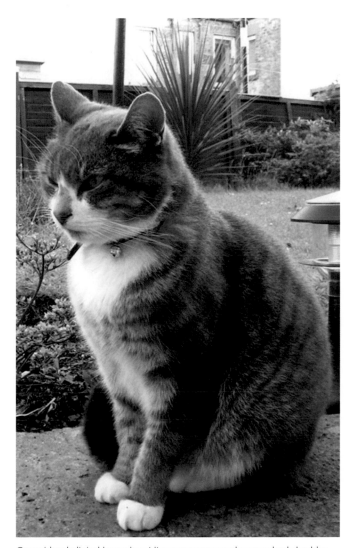

Cats with subclinical hyperthyroidism may appear to be completely healthy.

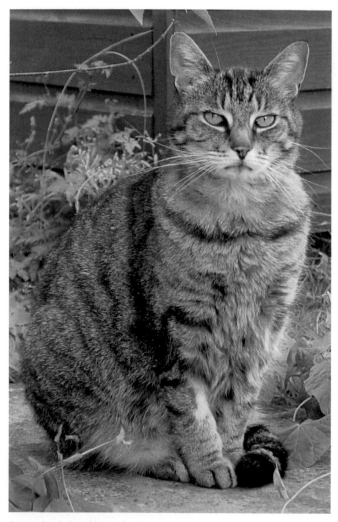

Cats with subclinical hyperthyroidism appear completely healthy but are more likely to develop overt hyperthyroidism in the next one to three years

- History and physical examination including bodyweight checks every 3-6 months. Presence of a goitre increases the likelihood of hyperthyroidism developing. However care should be taken not to over-interpret presence of a goitre since other causes of a nodule in the neck include non-functional thyroid nodules and enlargement of other (non-thyroid) tissue such as lymph glands. If weight loss is documented or other signs of hyperthyroidism appear, further tests should be done to look for hyperthyroidism

- Blood tests to check for hyperthyroidism every 6-12 months; sooner if any weight loss or other signs of illness are noticed. The most helpful blood tests to consider include haematology, serum biochemistry and total T4 tests as discussed later.

Are there other illnesses which can mimic hyperthyroidism?

You or your veterinarian may be suspicious of a diagnosis of hyperthyroidism if your cat is showing several of the clinical signs reported earlier. For example, weight loss in spite of a normal or increased appetite is one of the most common reasons that hyperthyroidism is suspected. However there are other illnesses which can produce similar symptoms – common examples would include:

- Polyphagia: an increased appetite can also be caused by illnesses such as diabetes mellitus ('sugar diabetes'), inflammatory bowel disease and some liver and pancreas problems

- Polydipsia and polyuria: an increased thirst and amount of urine produced can be seen with other illnesses including diabetes mellitus and chronic kidney disease

- Weight loss is a very common symptom of many illnesses and, even in an older cat, cannot be taken to indicate hyperthyroidism. Common causes of weight loss in older cats include chronic kidney disease, diabetes mellitus, cancer and bowel disorders

- Hyperactivity and restlessness can be seen with brain disorders (for example cancers) and with behavioural problems

- High blood pressure can be seen with a number of other problems but most common is chronic kidney disease

- Night crying can be seen with a number of illnesses including high blood pressure and brain disorders (for example cognitive dysfunction syndrome, a common cause of dementia in elderly cats).

How is hyperthyroidism diagnosed?

A vital starting component to making the diagnosis is taking a very thorough patient history as this is where clues of the underlying illness (such as polydipsia, polyuria and polyphagia) may become apparent. A patient history involves collecting as much information as possible about your cat and its illness.

After the history, a clinical examination is performed. During this procedure, further clues as to the cause of the illness (such as a heart murmur and rapid heart rate) may be detected.

In those cats where a diagnosis of hyperthyroidism is suspected on the basis of the history and/or clinical examination, it is likely that your veterinarian will recommend further tests to confirm the diagnosis. In most cats, measurement of thyroid hormone levels is sufficient to confirm the diagnosis although other tests are highly desirable, as discussed below.

An increased hunger can be seen with a number of medical conditions including diabetes mellitus, inflammatory bowel disease and hyperthyroidism.

1. **Blood hormone tests:** It is essential that the diagnosis of hyperthyroidism is confirmed on blood testing to ensure that the correct treatment is given. A diagnosis cannot be made on clinical grounds alone – for example, occasionally cats will have a goitre but will not be suffering from hyperthyroidism.

- Total thyroxine or total T4 levels: this test is most commonly used to confirm a diagnosis of hyperthyroidism. Levels of thyroxine, also known as T4 (or tetraiodothyronine), are increased in the vast majority of hyperthyroid cats so this is usually a very simple way of confirming the diagnosis and estimating its severity. The reference range for T4 levels is included in the table on page 22. Sometimes, particularly in early cases of hyperthyroidism, a normal total T4 value will be received in a cat that has this illness. This can be because levels of the hormone fluctuate

Diagnosis of hyperthyroidism is not always straightforward – sometimes it is necessary to do several tests to diagnose this condition.

and, in early disease, this variation from day to day may mean that sometimes the result is within the reference range. If your veterinarian suspects this possibility they may suggest repeating the total T4 test a few days or weeks later. In most cases this is the easiest way of confirming that the cat has hyperthyroidism. Presence of other illnesses (such as diabetes mellitus and chronic kidney disease) can reduce the blood levels of total T4 and in some cats this can reduce the T4 levels into the reference range (i.e. giving a falsely normal result). This phenomenon is known as 'sick euthyroid' and defines the situation where other illnesses suppress the levels of thyroid hormones. Where possible, treatment of any concurrent illness helps to increase the total T4 levels and can make diagnosis of hyperthyroidism more straightforward. Total T4 levels are used to monitor effectiveness of treatment for hyperthyroidism as discussed on pages 56–64.

■ Free thyroxine (fT4): in some cats, this additional test can be helpful in confirming the diagnosis of hyperthyroidism. Free T4 testing is more sensitive (identifies more hyperthyroid cats) than the total T4 test although it can occasionally falsely diagnose hyperthyroidism. For this reason the free T4 is not generally recommended as the first test for hyperthyroidism. The reference levels of free T4 are contained in the table on page 22. Some veterinarians routinely perform both a total and free T4 test when diagnosing hyperthyroidism in their patients. fT4 is not usually used for monitoring effectiveness of treatment for hyperthyroidism. Levels of fT4 can be affected by other illnesses and much less is known about the usefulness of this test in monitoring treated cats.

■ Thyroid function tests: very occasionally, the total T4 and free T4 results will not give a clear answer and other tests may be required to try and confirm a diagnosis of hyperthyroidism.

These tests include the T3 suppression and TRH stimulation tests. Of the two, the T3 suppression test is currently thought to be most reliable in diagnosing hyperthyroid cats. Results obtained with both of these tests can be affected by concurrent illnesses and this can make interpretation of results very difficult in some patients.

– T3 suppression test: in this test, cats are medicated for a few days with a form of thyroid hormone called T3. The T3 is given as an oral pill with the cat either in a veterinary hospital or at home. Blood samples are collected before T3 treatment is started and then a few days later, after a short course of treatment has been given. In normal cats, giving extra T3 switches off the thyroid so blood levels of thyroid hormones (total T4) fall. Hyperthyroid cats are resistant to the effects of T3 so their levels of T4 remain the same (or only fall very slightly)

– TRH stimulation test: in this test, cats are given a substance which, in normal cats, causes the release of T4 from the thyroid gland. The TRH is given as an intravenous injection (injection into a vein) and the test requires the cat to have a blood sample before the injection and four hours later. The second blood sample shows a rise in T4 levels in normal cats. Hyperthyroid cats resist the effects of TRH and so the T4 levels remain the same (or only slightly increase).

■ Thyroid stimulating hormone (TSH, thyrotropin) test: this test has been validated relatively recently in cats and can be helpful in diagnosing both hyperthyroidism and hypothyroidism. The currently available test is a canine assay (a test designed for use with dog blood so not ideal for feline blood); in the future a feline specific test may become available. TSH is a hormone which is produced in a part of the brain called the

Blood is normally collected from the jugular vein (i). The cephalic vein, in the front leg (ii) is another option.

pituitary gland. TSH stimulates production and release of thyroid hormones by the thyroid gland.

– Cats suffering from hyperthyroidism have low or undetectable levels of TSH. This test can be helpful in identifying cats suffering from sick euthyroidism where concurrent disease has suppressed levels of total T4 into the reference range. For example a total T4 in the upper half of the reference range in combination with a low TSH result is indicative of hyperthyroidism, especially if the cat is known to have concurrent disease such as chronic kidney disease

– A low TSH result may be useful in highlighting cats with subclinical hyperthyroidism which are more likely to develop hyperthyroidism in the following one to three years

– Measurement of TSH levels is not routinely performed in cats at the moment and low levels of TSH can be found in some healthy older cats. Therefore a single abnormal result should not be used to diagnose subclinical hyperthyroidism

– Occasionally, high-normal total T4 results (ie results at the top of the reference range) can be received in routine screening of apparently healthy cats (cats free of clinical signs). A normal TSH result can be helpful in ruling out hyperthyroidism as a diagnosis in some of these

– Cats suffering from hypothyroidism (an underactive thyroid gland) have high levels of TSH. Hypothyroidism is discussed in more detail on pages 50–52.

2. Blood tests: haematology (assessing the blood count, numbers and types of white blood cells and platelets) and biochemistry (assessing liver and kidney function, blood salt levels and protein levels) are recommended, where possible. Although these tests will not specifically diagnose hyperthyroidism, they are helpful in several ways:

■ Looking for clues of hyperthyroidism: for example, many cats with hyperthyroidism have increased blood levels of liver enzymes (for example ALT, ALP). This is a common way that hyperthyroid cats are picked up during routine screening tests – for example in an older cat having a blood test to check that they are well enough to have an anaesthetic for dental treatment. Other abnormalities that may be seen on routine haematology and biochemistry in a hyperthyroid cat include:

– A leucocytosis: increase in the total number of white blood cells

– An eosinopenia: a reduction in the number of eosinophils, a specific type of white blood cell

– Erythrocytosis: an increase in the total number of red blood cells and haemoglobin (Hb)

– Hyperphosphataemia: an increase in blood phosphate levels (usually mild)

– Hypokalaemia: a reduction in blood potassium levels (usually mild).

It is important to note that none of these changes are diagnostic for hyperthyroidism – all of the abnormalities listed above can occur with other illnesses.

■ Looking for evidence of concurrent illnesses. Concurrent illnesses can affect which treatment is recommended for a hyperthyroid cat and also the cat's likely long-term outlook (the prognosis). Identifying concurrent illnesses early ensures the best chance of managing these and giving your cat the best possible quality and length of life possible.

The most common concurrent illness seen is chronic kidney disease. Unfortunately the tests currently available to test for this are not perfect and it can be quite difficult to assess kidney function in hyperthyroid cats. For example the normal measures of kidney function – the protein breakdown products urea and creatinine, and urine concentration – can all be affected by thyroid disease:

– Urea tends to be high as a hyperthyroid cat often eats excessively and consumes lots of protein and this may falsely increase the worry that a hyperthyroid cat has kidney disease

– Creatinine tends to be low as hyperthyroid cats are thin and have very little muscle (creatinine comes from muscle turnover). This can be misleading by falsely suggesting that the cat has good kidney function

- The measure of urine concentration, urine specific gravity (USG), can be affected by thyroid disease. In healthy cats the USG is greater than 1.040. Concentrations below 1.035 are taken as one of the indications of kidney disease. In hyperthyroid cats, the ability to produce concentrated urine is compromised and USGs below this figure can be obtained from cats that have healthy kidneys. USG is discussed in more detail in the urinalysis section

- Also, the erythrocytosis seen in some hyperthyroid cats can 'hide' an anaemia (lack of red blood cells) that might be present in a cat with kidney disease.

Diabetes mellitus is another illness that is common in older cats. Clinical signs of diabetes mellitus and hyperthyroidism are often very similar, with an increased thirst and weight loss in spite of a good appetite being most common. Some cats suffer from both illnesses at the same time. Hyperthyroidism increases the likelihood of diabetes developing since thyroid hormones interfere with the way insulin (the hormone that regulates blood sugar levels) is able to work. This interference can lead to development of diabetes mellitus. In those cats that are already diabetic, subsequent development of hyperthyroidism can make management of their diabetes more difficult. Diagnosis of diabetes is often more difficult in hyperthyroid cats. Firstly, both conditions are often associated with similar biochemistry abnormalities (e.g. an increase in liver enzymes). Secondly, one of the diagnostic tests for diabetes mellitus (the fructosamine test) can be affected by hyperthyroidism. Fructosamine is a measure of the blood sugar levels over a period of one to two weeks and blood levels of fructosamine are high in cats with untreated diabetes mellitus. Hyperthyroid cats tend to have lower levels of fructosamine

> **Diabetes mellitus is another illness that is common in older cats. Clinical signs of diabetes mellitus and hyperthyroidism are often very similar, with an increased thirst and weight loss in spite of a good appetite being most common.**

due to their increased metabolic rate and this can sometimes be misleading by falsely suggesting that the cat is not diabetic. Diagnosis of hyperthyroidism can also be more difficult in diabetic cats since the thyroid hormone levels can be reduced by the presence of a concurrent illness.

- Establishing 'baseline' values. Many hyperthyroid cats will require at least short-term medication to treat their thyroid disease and whilst serious side-effects are rare, some of these can be detected when monitoring blood test results. It is therefore important to have pre-treatment or 'baseline' information available on each patient, where possible. Following treatment of hyperthyroidism, there may be a decline in kidney function. Unfortunately this is unpredictable and there are no tests that can be done before treatment is started that will tell you whether this is likely to occur. This issue is discussed in more detail on pages 31–32. Pre-treatment screening tests help to establish a baseline for monitoring kidney function once treatment is started.

Collection of blood samples should not be a stressful event for a cat. Blood is most easily collected from the jugular vein which is the largest vein and is located in the cat's neck. Alternatively blood can be collected from a cephalic vein which is a smaller vein, found on the front surface of the forelimbs or the medial saphenous vein which is found on the inside surface of the hind limbs.

Different laboratories have different reference ranges for blood test values and, different countries use different units which further confuses matters. The two types of unit measurements used are:

- Conventional units: used by some countries including the USA
- SI units: used by most countries including the UK

The table below gives a guide to the reference range levels which are likely to be normal for where you live. N.B. the reference range will vary slightly between laboratories so the following is just a rough guide:

Parameter	'Typical reference range' – Conventional units	'Typical reference range' – SI units
Urea	17 – 29 mg/dl	6 – 10 mmol/l
Creatinine	< 2 mg/dl	< 175 µmol/l
Phosphate	2.9 – 6.0 mg/dl	0.95 – 1.95 mmol/l
Potassium	4.0 – 5.0 mEq/l	4.0 – 5.0 mmol/l
Sodium	145 – 160 mEq/l	145 – 160 mmol/l
Calcium	8 – 10 mg/dl	2.0 – 2.5 mmol/l
Albumin	2.4 – 3.5 g/dl	24 – 35 g/l
Total protein	5.5 – 8.0 g/dl	55 – 80 g/l
Bicarbonate	18 – 24 mEq/l	18 – 24 mmol/l
Packed cell volume (PCV) or haematocrit	25 – 45 %	0.25 – 0.45
Haemoglobin (Hb)	0.8 – 1.5 g/dl	8 – 15 g/l
Alanine aminotransferase (ALT)	< 60 iu/l	< 60 iu/l
Alkaline phosphatase (ALP)	< 60 iu/l	< 60 iu/l
Cholesterol	85 – 155 mg/dl	2.2 – 4.0 mmol/l
Glucose	55 – 100 mg/dl	3.0 -5.5 mmol/l
Total Thyroxine (tT4)	1.5 – 3.5µg/dl	20 – 45 nmol/l
Free T4 (fT4) by equilibrium dialysis	1.0 – 4.0 ng/dl	10 – 50 pmol/l
Free T4 by chemiluminescent immunoassay (Idexx)	0.7-2.6ng/dl	9.0-35 pmol/l
TSH (canine assay)		0.03-0.15 ng/ml

mg/dl – milligrams per decilitre   µmol/l – micromoles per litre   g/dl – grams per decilitre
mmol/l – millimoles per litre   mEq/l – milliequivalents per litre   g/l – grams per litre.

A table with conversion factors for converting SI units to Conventional units (and vice versa) is contained in the Reference section (Section 5).

3. Urinalysis: analysis of a urine sample is very helpful in cats with hyperthyroidism although, as with haematology and biochemistry, this test will not confirm the diagnosis. The main usefulness of urinalysis is in:

- Checking for concurrent illnesses: Urinalysis can be helpful in diagnosing diabetes mellitus – diabetic cats will have glucose (sugar) present in their urine sample. Stress may also occasionally cause some glucose to be present in a urine sample. A urinalysis is also helpful in assessing your cat's ability to produce concentrated urine. Cats with severe chronic kidney disease will often produce dilute urine which can be identified on a specific gravity test. However, hyperthyroidism also reduces the cat's ability to produce concentrated urine – although not usually as severely - so this test is not always easy to interpret.

- Checking for urinary tract infections (UTIs): recent studies have shown that a significant proportion of cats with hyperthyroidism are vulnerable to UTIs. One study showed that 12% of hyperthyroid cats suffered from UTIs. Unfortunately, many cats with urinary infections do not show specific clinical signs (i.e. the infection is 'silent') and may only show vague clinical signs such as weight loss and lethargy. A small proportion of cats with urinary infections show clinical signs of cystitis including urgency to pass urine, passing small amounts of urine very frequently and passing bloody/smelly urine. It is important to identify and treat any of these additional problems, as it will help to make your cat feel as well as possible.

Urine samples can be collected in a variety of ways:

- **Cystocentesis**: this is the procedure by which urine is collected using a needle and syringe. The cat is gently held and the needle is passed through the skin of the tummy into the bladder. This is not a painful procedure and allows collection of a sterile (free from bacterial contamination) sample which is ideal for the tests needed.

- **Catheter samples**: urine can be collected using a catheter which is passed through the urethra (the tube from the outside of the cat to the bladder). Unfortunately this is not an appropriate technique for urine collection in most cats as it

This cat has glucose present in the urine – detected since the circled pad has changed in colour from pale aqua to dark brown.

If your cat is passing small amounts of bloody urine then this may be a sign of a bacterial urinary tract infection.

requires sedation (using drugs to provide a state of calm and muscle relaxation) or anaesthesia (using drugs to provide a state of unconsciousness, muscle relaxation and loss of pain sensation). A catheter is only appropriate as a method for urine collection if it needs to be placed for other reasons.

■ **Free catch samples**: urine can be collected from an empty litter tray or one containing non-absorbent cat litter. Lots of different types of non-absorbent cat litter are available (for example Mikki, KiT4Cat and Katkor brands) or cheaper alternatives can be used (e.g. clean aquarium gravel, chopped up plastic bags). Once the cat has urinated, the urine can be collected using a syringe or pipette. It is important that the sample is collected as soon as possible after urination. Free catch samples are acceptable for initial assessment. For example the refractometer test which determines the concentration of the urine is not affected by the method of collection. Free catch samples are not ideal

Cystocentesis is a commonly used technique to collect a urine sample. This is a procedure which is well tolerated by cats and can be done with them fully conscious, gently restrained by a nurse.

Non-absorbent cat litter can be used to collect urine samples at home or in the hospital.

for bacterial culture or sediment examination as they will be contaminated by bacteria and debris in the litter tray and on the cat's paws. Where possible a cystocentesis sample is best for bacterial culture and sediment examination.

Urine should be analysed as quickly as possible. Important urine tests in a cat with hyperthyroidism include:

■ **Specific gravity measurement**: A refractometer measures the urine specific gravity. Water has a specific gravity of 1.000. Normal cats usually produce urine with a specific gravity of at least 1.040. The lower the specific gravity, the more dilute the urine is. Most refractometers are designed for human urine and only measure to 1.050 so if the urine is more concentrated than this, the result will be reported as 'greater than 1.050'. Special veterinary refractometers are available in some practices and can accurately measure urine concentrations above 1.050. Cats with hyperthyroidism often have a slight reduction in their specific gravity – for example results between 1.030 and 1.040. Cats with severe kidney disease usually have a greater reduction in their specific gravity – for example results between 1.015 and 1.030.

■ **Urine dipstick** to check for sugar (glucose), assess the acidity of the urine (urine pH) and look for other abnormalities. Glucose is present in the urine of cats with diabetes mellitus (and sometimes in the urine of cats that are stressed). Some

Urine is analysed in a number of ways including:

i. 'Dipstick' tests (as in people to detect sugar and protein in the urine)

ii. Urine concentration using a refractometer. Normal cats usually produce concentrated urine with a specific gravity greater than 1.040

Hyperthyroidism and chronic kidney disease are examples of two illnesses which can reduce the urine specific gravity to below 1.040.

hyperthyroid cats have concurrent diabetes mellitus. Dipsticks have been designed for use with human urine so are not always as reliable when used with cat urine.

- **Sediment examination**: This involves microscopic examination of a urine sample for red and white blood cells, bacteria, crystals or other material. For example this can help to diagnose a urinary tract infection. Crystals are a normal finding in cat urine, especially if the cat is fed a dry diet and also if the sample is not analysed immediately. As the temperature of the urine cools (either at room temperature or in a refrigerator) crystals will form so their significance should not be over-estimated.

- **Bacterial culture** to see whether there is any evidence of infection. Ideally this test should be performed on urine collected by cystocentesis. When a bacterial infection is diagnosed by the laboratory they will do a sensitivity test (also referred to as a susceptibility test) to identify which antibiotics are likely to be most effective in treating the infection. This is a test which takes a few days to perform as bacterial colonies need time to grow.

4. **Thyroid scintigraphy**: This technique is also referred to as a technetium scan, isotope scan or radionuclide imaging. Scintigraphy is an imaging technique that can be very helpful in hyperthyroid cats. A short-acting injection of radioactive technetium is given to the cat. A few minutes later, the cat is sedated and placed on a gamma camera. The gamma camera produces a map of radioactivity in the cat's body. Technetium naturally concentrates in the thyroid gland so this allows it to be seen on the 'map' – even if it's very small. Scintigraphy is helpful in diagnosing hyperthyroidism (the thyroid will be more radioactive – 'hotter' – if it's diseased) and also locating the abnormal thyroid tissue (see pictures on page 26). It is most helpful in the following situations:

- Locating the abnormal thyroid tissue in hyperthyroid cats which do not have a goitre

- Locating the abnormal thyroid tissue in cats whose hyperthyroidism has recurred after surgical treatment

- Identifying whether the thyroid disease is affecting one or both of the thyroid lobes (uni- or bilateral disease)

- Identifying whether any ectopic thyroid tissue is affected

- Identifying whether a malignant thyroid carcinoma (cancer) has spread to other parts of the body

- The scan may be of help in deciding whether or not a malignant thyroid carcinoma will be amenable to treatment.

Scintigraphy helps to decide which treatment is most appropriate for the cat – for example, cats with diseased ectopic thyroid tissue cannot be treated surgically. The scan procedure only takes a few minutes to perform. Unfortunately scintigraphy is only available in a few centres in the UK and around the world.

Left: Scintigraphy can be used to locate the abnormal thyroid tissue which is 'hotter' (darker) on a scan. The cat is given an injection of radioactive technetium which concentrates in the thyroid gland. A picture is taken with the cat lying on their front. In this scan, one thyroid in the neck is very 'hot' due to unilateral hyperthyroidism.

Right: This thyroid scan shows that all of the abnormal thyroid tissue is within the chest cavity. This is due to ectopic disease.

What other tests are helpful in cats with hyperthyroidism?

1. Blood pressure measurement: This is recommended in all hyperthyroid cats since high blood pressure (systemic hypertension) is a known complication of this illness. Published reports of how commonly systemic hypertension is seen in hyperthyroid cats have varied enormously but most clinicians estimate that 15% of their hyperthyroid patients have high blood pressure. Systemic hypertension is often referred to as 'the silent killer' in people as it is common to show no

outward signs of this condition before severe problems strike. High blood pressure is especially damaging to the eyes, brain and nervous system, heart and kidneys. Some cats with high blood pressure will show clinical signs including:

- Eye problems such as bleeding into the eye, dilatation of the pupils (the black slit in the centre of the eye becomes very large and round), difficulty seeing and blindness. Sudden blindness is an emergency – prompt treatment can be successful in returning some vision although, sadly, many cats will remain blind for the rest of their life. Examples of eye problems can be seen on pages 60 and 64

- Neurological signs such as collapse and seizures (fits) or behavioural changes (e.g. pacing aimlessly, night-time miaowing or yowling, showing signs of dementia)

- Damage to the heart resulting in development of a heart murmur and, in a very small number of cats, heart failure. Signs of heart failure most commonly include lethargy and breathlessness

- Damage to the kidneys may worsen or cause chronic kidney disease. Signs of kidney disease include a loss of appetite, weight loss, lethargy and an increased thirst and volume of urine produced.

Systemic hypertension is a very serious condition and it is vital that it is diagnosed and treated quickly and effectively. Systemic hypertension is diagnosed by measuring blood pressure – this is a procedure which can be done in most practices. If facilities are not available to measure blood pressure, then your veterinarian may refer you to another practice or to a specialist so that this test can be done. Examination of the eyes can be extremely helpful when checking for signs of hypertension – your veterinarian

Blood pressure is most accurately measured using a Doppler machine and is a procedure which is very well tolerated by fully conscious cats. A cuff attached to a pressure gauge (called a sphygmomanometer) is placed on a forelimb or the tail; a separate sensor (the Doppler probe) is used to detect the pulse below the cuff. The cuff is inflated until the pulse signal disappears and then deflated slowly. The systolic blood pressure (higher of the two blood pressure readings we get when our own blood pressure is measured) is the pressure at which the pulse is first detectable.

may be able to see abnormalities such as bleeding into the eye or retinal detachment (where the retina – the 'seeing' layer of tissue at the back of the eye – lifts off). It is currently recommended that systolic blood pressure (the higher of the two blood pressure readings) is kept below 160 mmHg (mmHg is the abbreviation for millimetres of mercury) in cats with hyperthyroidism. Readings persistently above 180-190 mmHg especially increase the risk of potentially permanent organ damage. The most helpful

drugs for treating high blood pressure are amlodipine (a human drug manufactured by Pfizer as Istin in the UK, Norvasc in the US) and Angiotensin Converting Enzyme (ACE) inhibitors such as benazepril (for example Fortekor, manufactured by Novartis).

2. Diagnostic imaging: Diagnostic imaging is the term that refers to imaging techniques such as radiography (x-rays) and ultrasound. Radiographs can be helpful in identifying a number of problems:

- Heart problems can be seen as a consequence of hyperthyroidism and, in a very small number of cats, this leads to congestive heart failure. Affected cats may have abnormalities visible on radiographs including enlargement of the heart, congestion of the lungs and presence of free fluid in the chest and/or abdomen
- Concurrent illnesses such as cancers may be visible on x-rays of the chest and/or abdomen
- In those cats where the goitre cannot be felt, x-rays can sometimes be helpful in locating the abnormal thyroid tissue.

In most cats sedation is needed to obtain good quality radiographs of the chest and abdomen.

Ultrasound examination can be very helpful in some patients including the following situations:

- In those cats with a very large goitre, ultrasound may identify that the lump is fluid filled (the medical term for this is 'cystic')
- Ultrasound of the heart is helpful in assessing the severity of any heart disease present in a hyperthyroid cat. A heart ultrasound test is called echocardiography or an echocardiogram. Most commonly, the left ventricle chamber of the heart will

A chest x-ray can be helpful in diagnosing heart problems associated with hyperthyroidism. This cat has been sedated and is being positioned for a dorsoventral chest x-ray.

be thickened (referred to as left ventricular hypertrophy, LVH) and the left atrium may be enlarged (dilated). Sometimes, this condition is referred to as hyperthyroid heart disease or, less accurately, as hypertrophic cardiomyopathy (HCM). True HCM is a separate condition where there is no known cause to the heart changes. In many hyperthyroid cats, the LVH does not cause significant heart problems and there is no heart failure. The changes to the heart chambers often cause a murmur or a 'gallop rhythm' which can be heard when listening to the chest with a stethoscope. Cats with a gallop rhythm have three or four audible heart sounds instead of the normal two (lub-dub), thus sounding similar to a galloping horse. Although not always an indicator of disease, gallop rhythms are most often heard in cats with heart disease (cardiomyopathy) or high blood pressure. A gallop rhythm is one indication that

the heart is not able to fill with blood as well as it should. A small percentage of hyperthyroid cats will suffer from congestive heart failure where the heart is no longer able to cope with its increased workload. Heart failure can cause congestion of the blood vessels in the lungs, pulmonary oedema (fluid within the lung tissue) and fluid production in the chest and/or abdominal cavity. Fluid in the chest cavity is called a pleural effusion; fluid in the abdomen is called ascites. The most common signs of heart failure are breathlessness due to pulmonary oedema and/or a pleural effusion

- Ultrasound of any abnormalities found on an x-ray can help to define what these are and their significance to the cat's health

- Ultrasound of the larynx can be helpful in diagnosing laryngeal paralysis. This is a rare side-effect seen in some cats with very large goitres and in other cats following surgery to remove a thyroid mass. Cats with laryngeal paralysis may have breathing difficulties, a change in voice (altered pitch to their meow) and a cough

- In some situations, a screening ultrasound of the abdomen is done to look for concurrent illnesses which might be difficult to diagnose using other techniques.

Ultrasound does not usually require sedation or anaesthesia.

3. Electrocardiogram (ECG): in some cats, an ECG might be helpful in assessing the severity of the heart disease associated with their hyperthyroidism. For example, the heart rate should be very regular – like a metronome – but if an abnormal heart rhythm (arrhythmia) is heard when listening with a stethoscope, an ECG can be helpful in understanding the cause of this and whether it needs treatment.

4. **Thyroid biopsy and cytology**: A biopsy involves collection and laboratory analysis of a sample of tissue such as the thyroid. Biopsies can be collected in three main ways:

■ Fine needle aspirate (FNA): the technique by which a sample of cells is extracted from the thyroid using a needle inserted through the skin. This procedure is relatively safe ('non-invasive') but often will not give enough information as to the precise nature of the disease

■ Needle core biopsy: the technique by which a cylinder of tissue is obtained using a special needle inserted through the skin (under the guidance of ultrasound). This provides more tissue than an FNA but even so may not provide sufficient tissue to always make an accurate diagnosis. Needle core biopsies can only be done on very large goitres – they are not safe to perform on a smaller goitre. If done on a normal or small goitre, the biopsy needle risks causing damage to other important structures in the area of the thyroid such as blood vessels and nerves

■ Surgical biopsy: the technique by which the whole thyroid (excisional biopsy) or a portion of the gland (incisional biopsy) is removed via surgery. This provides the best sample of tissue for a pathologist to examine but involves general anaesthesia (deep sedation can be sufficient for the other two techniques) and the associated surgical and anaesthetic risks.

In general, biopsies are not commonly performed as:

■ In most cats with thyroid disease, the biopsy results will not affect the treatment that the cat needs.

■ The procedure requires sedation or anaesthesia which can be risky in some patients.

> **If other illnesses are suspected then your vet may recommend that additional tests are performed.**

A thyroid biopsy is indicated in those cats where a malignant thyroid tumour (cancer) is suspected. This is since the treatment required for these patients is very different to that for 'routine' cases and prompt treatment improves the long-term outlook with this illness. Examples of situations where a biopsy might be indicated therefore include:

■ Where malignant thyroid disease is suspected on clinical examination, for example if the thyroid lump feels very adherent (stuck) to the tissues of the neck

■ Where hyperthyroidism has recurred following previous surgery – this is another situation when a malignant thyroid problem could be to blame

■ In cats with multiple thyroid lumps. In this situation it is not always easy to determine if all of the lumps are thyroid or whether other tissues (such as the parathyroid glands and lymph tissue) could be involved

■ In cats where scintigraphy has been performed and has suggested that the disease could be cancerous.

Where possible, the thyroid tissue removed from cats having surgical treatment for 'routine' hyperthyroidism (the benign disease) should be sent to a pathologist for analysis to double check that a malignant cancer is not being ignored.

5. Other tests: If other illnesses are suspected then your veterinarian may recommend that additional tests are performed. For example, if the liver enzymes are very high then your veterinarian may suggest that a liver ultrasound examination is performed. In cats that have a goitre but normal thyroid hormone levels, other tests suggested may include blood calcium and phosphate levels and assessment of parathyroid gland function.

What does treatment of a hyperthyroid cat involve?

The approach to treatment of hyperthyroidism involves:

1. Providing treatment for the thyroid **disease:** This will be discussed in more detail below.

2. Providing treatment for known complications of thyroid **disease**: Some hyperthyroid cats need additional medication for complications associated with their hyperthyroidism. For example, high blood pressure (systemic hypertension) is seen in a significant proportion of hyperthyroid cats and requires specific treatment with drugs like amlodipine (a human drug manufactured by Pfizer in the UK as Istin, Norvasc in the US) and/or ACE inhibitors such as benazepril (for example Fortekor, manufactured by Novartis). Cats suffering from hyperthyroidism are more vulnerable to acquiring bacterial urinary tract infections, especially if they are also suffering from chronic kidney disease or diabetes mellitus. If your cat has been diagnosed with a bacterial urinary tract infection then a course of antibiotics will be recommended. The type of antibiotic and length of course depends on factors including the type of infection and results of the bacterial culture and sen-

Thoracocentesis (draining the chest) may be needed in cats suffering from congestive heart failure associated with their hyperthyroidism. The cat pictured here was suffering from a condition called pyothorax which is caused by an infection.

sitivity test. The sensitivity test evaluates the ability of several different antibiotics to slow or stop the growth of the bacteria in laboratory conditions. Where concurrent kidney disease is also present, it is not unusual to prescribe a four to six week course of antibiotics. Successful treatment of some infections requires repeat and/or prolonged courses of treatment and your veterinarian may recommend that repeat bacterial cultures are performed on urine samples periodically to monitor progress. Unfortunately antibiotic resistance can occur necessitating a change in the type of antibiotic prescribed.

Hyperthyroid cats with heart complications may need additional treatment such as:

Antithyroid medication is rapidly effective in reducing blood thyroid hormone levels to the normal range.

- Diuretics to help treat congestive heart failure, for example, furosemide (Dimazon, Frusedale, Frusecare and Lasix are examples of trade names of this drug)
- Angiotensin Converting Enzyme inhibitors (ACE inhibitors) such as benazepril (for example Fortekor, manufactured by Novartis) to help manage heart failure
- Beta blockers such as propranolol and atenolol to help reduce the heart rate to more acceptable levels if tachycardia (a racing heart rate) is a problem.

Drainage of the pleural effusion via a procedure called thoracocentesis. This may be done with your cat fully conscious or after sedation. Thoracocentesis involves inserting a needle into the chest cavity so that fluid can be removed.

3. **Providing treatment for additional concurrent illnesses**: Since hyperthyroidism is a condition which is common in older cats, it is not unusual for them to have more than one medical problem. Other common illnesses in older cats include chronic kidney disease and diabetes mellitus ('sugar diabetes'). If present, these conditions also require treatment.

How is hyperthyroidism treated?

There are four main treatment options for hyperthyroid cats:

- Medical treatment: prescribing antithyroid drugs which block production of thyroid hormones
- Nutritional management: exclusive feeding of an iodine-restricted food which limits the production of thyroid hormones
- Surgical treatment: removal of the diseased thyroid tissue
- Radioiodine: a form of radiotherapy that is able to treat abnormal thyroid tissue.

Other than nutritional management, all of these treatments are also used in people with thyroid problems. For example, 80-90% of hyperthyroid people are cured by a single, tiny dose of radioactive iodine (radioiodine).

All treatments for hyperthyroidism have the potential to worsen kidney function. This is because the hyperthyroid condition increases blood flow to the kidneys. When the hyperthyroidism is treated, the blood flow to the kidneys decreases. For many hyperthyroid cats, this return to normality is not associated with kidney problems. However, in up to 20% of patients, this

All treatments for hyperthyroidism have the potential to worsen kidney function.

reduction in blood flow has the potential to 'unmask' or reveal kidney disease that was not previously known about and to worsen pre-existing kidney disease. Assessing kidney function in hyperthyroid cats is difficult for many reasons, and it is not possible to predict which patients will deteriorate into chronic kidney disease following treatment of their thyroid disease. For this reason, most clinicians prefer to treat all hyperthyroid cats with medical management or an iodine-restricted food in the first instance. The main advantage of these options is that they are reversible – in other words, if the kidney function deteriorates, the management can be reduced or stopped to help the cat to cope again.

If a cat is known to have kidney disease before nutritional or medical treatment is started then your veterinarian may recommend that your cat's kidney values are monitored more frequently. In those cats treated with antithyroid medications, a lower dose of medication may be recommended initially. If any problems are seen, then the dose of treatment can be lowered or even stopped (see page 54 for more information).

Medical treatment is currently the most commonly used treatment – almost all hyperthyroid cats will initially be prescribed a course of antithyroid drugs even if they go on to have either surgical treatment or radioiodine. Medical treatment can be used on its own as a lifelong treatment for hyperthyroidism. A UK competition identified a cat called Sasha as the longest treated cat with antithyroid medication. Sasha had been receiving Felimazole (one of the UK veterinary licensed antithyroid medications) for seven years at the time of the competition.

Medical treatment of hyperthyroidism

The class of antithyroid medications most commonly used include the thioureylenes (also known as thionamides) carbimazole and methimazole (also known as thiamazole). A third thioureylene, propylthiouracil, is used much less frequently since it causes more side-effects than the other drugs.

Carbimazole is rapidly converted into methimazole by the body so both of these drugs work in the same way. Methimazole blocks the production of the thyroid hormones T4 and T3 within the thyroid gland. The blood levels of thyroid hormones fall over a period of a few days to a few weeks (depending on how high they were to start with) until they are back in the reference range. Thioureylenes are not able to cure the thyroid disease. Continued therapy with carbimazole or methimazole is needed to ensure that the blood levels stay within the reference range. Thioureylenes can be used for short periods to stabilise patients prior to curative treatments (such as radioiodine and surgery) or can be used for the rest of the cat's life to keep the thyroid disease in remission (under control).

Both carbimazole and methimazole can be given as oral tablets, usually once or twice a day. In a number of countries (including North America, Australia, the UK and some parts of Europe), transdermal preparations of thioureylenes are available from some pharmacists. Transdermal preparations come as a skin cream which is usually applied to the inside of the cat's ear (a hairless area). The medication is absorbed through the skin and into the blood stream. Transdermal antithyroid medications can take longer to be effective than the oral forms. Transdermal medications are controversial – there is much less evidence to demonstrate their effectiveness. The skin normally forms a barrier to stop substances from entering the body so this might not always be a good way of delivering a drug to the blood stream.

There are no licensed (veterinary authorised) transdermal antithyroid medications available in the UK so these can only be used under Cascade regulations (page 37).

Advantages of thioureylenes include:

- The drugs are readily available through all vet practices so it's easy to get hold of them and start the treatment

- This treatment is initially less expensive than the curative treatment options (surgery and radioiodine) although lifelong treatment can be as expensive (or more expensive, if your cat lives a long time on this treatment)

- The treatment starts to work very quickly and most cats have normal blood levels of thyroid hormones within three weeks of starting the therapy

- Most cats suffer no side-effects of treatment, even with very long-term use. Many cats will remain stable for years when treated with these drugs

- The treatment can be titrated 'to effect' – in other words, the dose of treatment can be varied to suit the individual cat. This is especially helpful in some cats that have concurrent illnesses, most important of which is chronic kidney disease

- The treatment is reversible which is an advantage in cats with concurrent kidney disease where any treatment for hyperthyroidism can cause a worsening in their kidney function

- Medical management is a good way of stabilising a patient in preparation for surgical treatment or whilst awaiting

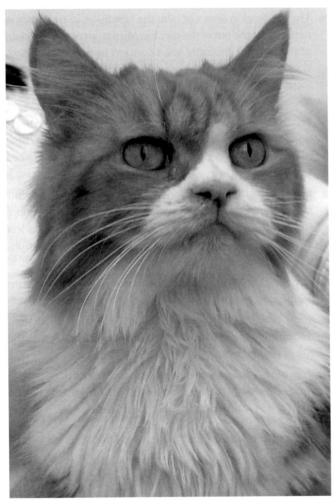

Most hyperthyroid cats treated with antithyroid medication suffer no side-effects of treatment, even with very long-term use.

stable (euthyroid), a proportion of cats can be maintained on once a day treatment although others will need to remain on twice daily treatment. Felimazole can be given with or without food although you should try and be consistent in how you medicate your cat. For those cats that are difficult to medicate orally, hiding the pill in a small amount of food can be helpful. Since methimazole is a bitter tasting drug, the pill should not be crushed in the food. Occasionally this is necessary to achieve medication – where it is done, the advice below should be followed

■ Carbimazole is manufactured in the UK as the veterinary licensed product Vidalta by MSD Animal Health; and as a human licensed product NeoMercazole by Amdipharm in the UK and some other countries. Carbimazole is a tasteless drug so does not normally come in a sugar coated form. Vidalta is a 'sustained release' preparation which means that the carbimazole is slowly released from the tablet. Because of this, Vidalta is only needed once a day or on alternate days. Standard carbimazole preparations (including the human preparation NeoMercazole) usually have to be given two to three times a day to be effective. Since Vidalta is a sustained release product the pill needs to be taken whole – if crushed the drug will all be released immediately and not last for 24 hours. If crushing the pill is necessary, Vidalta should be given twice daily (giving half the daily dose on each occasion). The absorption of Vidalta is affected by whether or not the cat has eaten so it is suggested that a stable routine is kept as to whether the tablet is given with or without food. Tablets should be given at the same time each day.

Advice on crushing methimazole and carbimazole in food:

Although not ideal, occasionally crushing methimazole or carbimazole is sometimes necessary to achieve medication. When you have to do this, you should wear gloves when crushing the pills since some people can be sensitive to antithyroid drugs. The crushed pill should be given in the smallest amount of food possible to try and ensure that the whole dose is eaten rather than being left in the food. Pregnant women should wear gloves when handling antithyroid drugs. Crushing medication constitutes 'off license' use of a veterinary authorised product and is not recommended unless this is the only way of successfully medicating your cat.

Information and tips on giving pills can be found on pages 36–40.

In the UK, strict laws exist to control the prescription of drugs to pets. These laws are aimed at protecting animals from medications which may be either unsafe or ineffective (or both). Under the Cascade system, veterinarians are obliged to prescribe veterinary licensed or 'authorised' preparations (drugs which have been designed for use in animals and which have been studied in animals) where these exist. If there is no medicine authorised for treatment of a specific condition in a particular species of animal then it is legal to use alternative treatments. When this is done, a strict sequence must be followed as below:

1. The first choice is a veterinary medicine authorised in the UK for use in another animal species

2. If this is not available then a medicine authorised in the UK for human use OR a veterinary medicine from another country can be imported under special import certificate

3. If neither of the above are possible then a veterinarian, pharmacist or other 'appropriate' person can prepare a medicine for use in a patient.

More detailed information can be read on: www.noahcompendium.co.uk/Compendium/Overview/-45043.html.

Treatment monitoring on thioureylene therapy

It is normal for treated cats to be reassessed around three weeks after starting therapy. At this time, the thyroid hormone levels are checked to see if your cat is on an adequate dose of treatment and additional tests are done to check for evidence of any side-effects such as kidney problems. Further monitoring tests are discussed on pages 56–59.

Other antithyroid medical agents

Very occasionally, other medical agents may be recommended for your cat. In general these are not as effective as the thioureylenes but may be recommended for cats that have suffered severe side-effects. In most cases, the drugs listed below are only effective as a short-term treatment before surgery or radioiodine therapy can be performed:

■ Stable iodine: this therapy can provide some short-term assistance in treating hyperthyroid cats by temporarily blocking production and release of thyroid hormones by the thyroid gland. Iodine tends to only be effective for up to a couple of weeks so is most helpful in stabilising a patient prior to surgery

- Calcium ipodate and iopanoic acid: these substances work by inhibiting conversion of T4 to T3. T3 is the more potent of the two thyroid hormones. Ipodate may also have some other effects, including blocking T3 receptors which stops T3 from having an effect on tissues

- Potassium iodate: this substance works by blocking the thyroid gland's ability to take up iodine and therefore helps to reduce blood levels of thyroid hormones. Some cats treated with this drug will suffer with an upset tummy; reducing the dose of drug can help to control this. Potassium iodate has been used successfully in combination with propranolol (see below) in stabilising hyperthyroid cats prior to surgery

- Beta blockers: drugs such as atenolol and propranolol can help stabilise hyperthyroid cats by slowing their heart rate and improving heart function. Beta blockers can also help treat some of the signs of anxiety and nervousness shown in some hyperthyroid cats. Propranolol has been used successfully in combination with potassium iodate in stabilising hyperthyroid cats prior to surgery.

None of the treatments listed above are veterinary licensed for treatment of hyperthyroid cats.

What is the best way to medicate my cat?

An illustrated guide on giving pills to a cat is on page 39. The Useful website section also contains a link to a video showing how to give pills and capsules to cats. Tablets should be given at the same time each day. If twice daily treatment is required it should be given as close to 12 hours apart as is practically possible. Three times a day medication should ideally be given eight hours apart. After any tab-

(i) Syringing a small amount of water after giving a pill or capsule helps the medication to travel to the stomach quickly and without causing any irritation to the oesophagus (food pipe). Alternatively (ii) a small amount of butter can be put on the cat's nose – licking this off also helps any pills and capsules to travel quickly to the stomach.

Medicating cats with pills or tablets

(i) try and ensure that your cat remains calm and relaxed; (ii) and (iii) the person restraining the cat gently holds the front legs so that they cannot come up and prevent pills being given or scratch you; (iv) and (v) make your forefingers and thumb into an arch shape and place this over the head holding the bony angles of the jaw firmly (this should not hurt your cat at all); (vi) tip your cat's head back gently so that the nose points to the ceiling; (vii) holding the pill between your thumb and forefinger gently open the jaw using your third finger; (viii) place the pill as far to the back of the mouth as possible; (ix) release your cat's head and allow them to swallow naturally, (x) syringe a small amount of water after giving the pill or allow your cat to have something to eat. (xi)–(xv) If your cat is very wriggly then placing them between your legs whilst you kneel on the floor or wrapping in a towel can help.

let or capsule medication is given the cat should be offered food or given a small amount of water (for example 1-5 ml of water by syringe) to encourage the tablet to travel to the stomach. This is to prevent tablets or capsules from sitting in the food pipe (oesophagus) for prolonged periods where they can cause irritation and potentially serious and long-lasting problems such as strictures (scarring and narrowing of the food pipe).

For those cats that are difficult to medicate orally, hiding the pill in a small amount of food can be helpful. Some cats enjoy treats such as soft cheese, butter or tuna and the pill can be hidden in here. Alternatively, you can try pill-hiding treats which are available from veterinarians and some pet shops – these include brands like Pill Pockets (manufactured by Greenies), Webbox cat treats (manufactured by Pets Choice Ltd.) and Tab Pockets (manufactured by Royal Canin).

Cats receiving multiple therapies can be difficult to medicate. Medicating with multiple drugs can be made easier by using empty gelatine capsules available from a veterinarian or pharmacist. The capsule is opened, the appropriate drugs are added and then the capsule is closed again. This means that it is possible to dose a cat with two or more medicines in one go – likely to be much more popular with the cat than giving multiple pills. Giving multiple medications can increase the risk of side-effects through drug interactions which is something for you and your veterinarian to discuss and be aware of when working out a treatment regime for your cat. If you are finding it difficult to medicate your cat ask your veterinarian to prioritise which treatments are most important so that you can ensure that your cat is getting the most important ones everyday.

Nutritional management of hyperthyroidism

In 2011, information started to emerge in the veterinary scientific journals about the use of an iodine-restricted food as a new way to control thyroid hormone levels in hyperthyroid cats. Several short scientific publications reported that exclusive feeding of an iodine-restricted cat food was successful in managing hyperthyroidism.

Production of thyroid hormone requires iodine molecules therefore limiting the amount of iodine fed reduces the amount of thyroid hormone that can be produced and released by the thyroid gland.

Blood levels of total thyroxine (total T4) are reported to decrease within 3 weeks of the cat exclusively eating an iodine-restricted food. No adverse effects have been reported when feeding an iodine-restricted food although the same concerns over renal function (pages 31–32) would exist with this management option as is the case with all other treatment modalities for hyperthyroidism.

Patient and care provider compliance is essential to the success of this approach – deviations from the recommended feeding can allow 'escape' of thyroid control. The food is only effective if used as the sole source of nutrition. Carers therefore need to be aware that their cat must not be allowed treats or other supplemental foods. Food bowls should not be used for other foods (for example in the case of multicat households) and should be thoroughly cleaned before use. Carers should also be advised to consult with their veterinarian regarding any supplements or other medications that their cat may be receiving. For example,

Feeding an iodine-restricted food is a reversible management option for hyperthyroidism.

change in food. For example offer a spoonful of the new food on day one increasing this amount over the following few days whilst decreasing the amount of the 'old' food offered until the cat is only offered the new food. Most cats take 5-7 days to transition to a new food but some cats may take several weeks to achieve this. If your cat refuses to eat the new food or you are at all concerned, contact your veterinarian for further advice. Some cats are very fussy about what foods they eat and this may mean that they will not accept an iodine-restricted food.

Can cats with chronic kidney disease and hyperthyroidism be managed with an iodine-restricted food?

The currently available iodine-restricted food is phosphate restricted and moderate in protein, making it an acceptable nutrition for cats with mild to moderate chronic kidney disease (IRIS stages 1-2; blood creatinine concentration less than 249 µmol/l or 2.8 mg/dl). For cats with more severe chronic kidney disease (IRIS stages 3-4; blood creatinine concentration greater than 249 µmol/l or 2.8 mg/dl), a food specially formulated for cats with kidney disease may be more appropriate in addition to medical management of the hyperthyroidism. Management of hyperthyroidism in cats with concurrent chronic kidney disease is discussed in more detail on page 54.

some pill pockets (e.g. Greenies® and most pet treats) contain iodine and therefore cannot be given to patients receiving an iodine-restricted food. It is not currently known whether iodine levels in tap water in some areas may pose a problem to control; offering deiodinised mineral water may be a safer option, especially in coastal areas where iodine content is likely to be higher.

Transition to the new food should be done gradually, over a few days, to minimise any gastrointestinal upsets associated with a

Can healthy cats safely eat an iodine-restricted food?

It is not recommended that healthy cats are fed an iodine-restricted food. There are some concerns that feeding an iodine deficient food could be one factor responsible for triggering development of hyperthyroidism. The food is termed an 'iodine-restricted' food and whilst no clinical signs of deficiency have been documented feeding this food exclusively to healthy cats for a period of one year, it is not recommended that this is done. In multicat homes where one cat is receiving an iodine-restricted food it is suggested that the remaining cats are fed their standard nutrition. Iodine-restricted foods are contra-indicated (not recommended) in queens (pregnant or lactating female cats) and growing kittens.

Many of the advantages of feeding an iodine-restricted food are similar to those for antithyroid medications – for example no anaesthesia or surgery is required and the food is readily available to most veterinary practices. Other advantages are:

- In cats happy to accept this food as their sole nutrition, the majority should achieve euthyroidism (have normal blood levels of thyroid hormones) without the need for additional antithyroid medication

- It starts to work very quickly: within three to four weeks, many cats are euthyroid (in the remaining cats, euthyroidism should be achieved within 12 weeks of exclusively feeding the iodine-restricted food)

- No side-effects which can develop after treatment with antithyroid medications (discussed on page 34) have been reported with this management option other than worsening or 'unmasking' of renal disease which is a potential with all treatments for hyperthyroidism (discussed on pages 31–32)

- In cats suffering renal complications following management of their hyperthyroidism with an iodine-restricted food, the food can be withdrawn. In other words, this management option is completely reversible

- In cats accepting this food, it is possible to manage hyperthyroidism for several years – the longest reported case so far has been managed for over 5 years whilst receiving an iodine-restricted food as the sole management for their hyperthyroidism

- The food can be used to stabilise cats suffering from hyperthyroidism prior to more curative treatments such as thyroid surgery (discussed on pages 43–47) or radioiodine (discussed on pages 47–49). It is recommended that management with the iodine-restricted food is withdrawn two weeks before treatment with radioiodine

- It is initially less expensive than the curative treatment options (surgery and radioiodine) although lifelong nutritional management may be expensive, depending on how long your cat lives

- Unlike medical treatments for hyperthyroidism, there is no potential for drug-related side-effects

- Filling a bowl with catfood is much easier than dosing a cat with antithyroid medication. This makes an iodine-restricted food a good option for elderly or disabled carers who find giving medication difficult.

Many of the disadvantages are similar to those for antithyroid medications – for example if this is to be used as the sole management, it will be needed for the remainder of the cat's life. Once management with an iodine-restricted food is stopped, the hyperthyroidism will recur (typically within a few days). Other disadvantages are:

- As with medical treatments for hyperthyroidism, monitoring is required to assess the cat's thyroid, renal status and blood pressure whilst receiving the food

- Cats receiving an iodine-restricted food cannot receive other foods or treats since these can interfere with the control of their hyperthyroidism

- In cats that frequently hunt and eat their prey, it may be difficult to manage their hyperthyroidism with an iodine-restricted food as ingested prey species may contain high levels of iodine

- An iodine-restricted food is not recommended as the sole food for healthy cats living in the same household as a cat with hyperthyroidism – these cats should receive their normal food

- Not all cats will accept an iodine-restricted food as their sole nutrition

- A small proportion of cats may not respond to an iodine-restricted food for other reasons.

Can cats that have been stabilised using antithyroid medications be transitioned onto an iodine-restricted food?

It is possible to transition cats receiving medical management of their hyperthyroidism on to an iodine-restricted food. Current recommendations are to stop antithyroid medications when first starting to feed the iodine-restricted food. Check-ups are recommended at the same frequency and time points as for those cats receiving an iodine-restricted food immediately following diagnosis, as discussed on pages 59–62.

Once the cat has been anaesthetised and the neck clipped and prepared for surgery, it may be possible to see the thyroid mass/masses in the neck. The cat shown had 2 thyroid carcinoma masses which are indicated with black arrows. The jugular vein is also visible (red arrow)

Surgical treatment of hyperthyroidism

Surgical treatment of hyperthyroidism involves removing the abnormal thyroid tissue. This procedure is called a thyroidectomy. Thyroid surgery can be unilateral (removing the abnormal thyroid gland on one side only) or bilateral (removing both abnormal thyroid glands). A number of different procedures have been described in cats with some surgeons preferring certain methods over others. Commonly performed techniques include the modified intra- and extra-capsular thyroidectomies.

Surgery requires anaesthesia of the patient, so where at all possible, your cat will be stabilised medically or by using an iodine-

restricted food before surgery is done. This is to reduce the risks of anaesthesia that are present in a cat with hyperthyroidism.

The ideal surgery:

- Removes all of the abnormal thyroid tissue leaving no 'remnants' that could possibly re-grow

- Does not remove or damage adjacent tissues. Of particular importance are:

  - The parathyroid glands: these small glands are located very close to the thyroid tissue and help to control blood levels of calcium. Two pairs of parathyroid gland are present in each cat – one pair lying outside the thyroid gland and the other pair lying inside the capsule that surrounds the thyroid. If these delicate structures are damaged or removed during thyroid surgery, affected cats can suffer from hypocalcaemia (low blood calcium levels) which can be fatal if not treated. This condition is called hypo parathyroidism. Since this is one of the most common side-effects of surgery it is discussed separately below

– The sympathetic nervous system: nerves involved in this part of the nervous system pass close to the thyroid glands and can be damaged during surgery. Affected cats can develop temporary or permanent Horner's syndrome (see right). This is recognised as a droopy upper eyelid, smaller pupil, a sunken eye (ptosis) and protrusion of the third eyelid (sometimes referred to as the Haws or nictitating membrane). This is a very rare potential complication of thyroid surgery and is usually temporary although it may take weeks or months to resolve

– The recurrent laryngeal nerve: this is one of the nerves that supplies the larynx (voice box). Temporary or permanent damage can occur during surgery and is called laryngeal paralysis (paralysis of the larynx). Affected cats may have voice changes, develop noisy breathing or a cough and can have difficulty breathing. In severe cases, surgery may be required to treat the laryngeal paralysis. This is a very rare, but sometimes fatal, potential complication of thyroid surgery

– Arteries and veins to and from the head and neck area: damage to these blood vessels can cause bruising of the tissue which may be visible. It is extremely rare to get any more serious side-effects associated with blood loss.

Horner's syndrome is a rare, and often temporary, complication that can be seen with thyroidectomy. Affected cats have a droopy upper eyelid, smaller pupil, sunken eye and protrusion of the third eyelid on the affected side. This cat has left-sided Horner's.

Advantages of surgical treatment include:

■ This is a curative procedure in those patients where it is possible to remove all of the abnormal thyroid tissue. After surgery, treated cats should no longer need antithyroid medication or an iodine-restricted food

■ Surgery can be done quickly and most veterinarians are very confident and competent in doing this operation.

Disadvantages of surgical treatment include:

- Your cat may need to be hospitalised for a few days for monitoring after surgery

- Anaesthesia is required and this can be a problem in some cats – for example those with heart or kidney disease. An untreated hyperthyroid cat is more sensitive to certain medications used in anaesthesia so achieving control of the hyperthyroidism before surgery is very important

- The procedure is only possible if the abnormal thyroid tissue is within the neck and therefore easily accessible by the surgeon. For those cats with ectopic thyroid tissue, other treatment methods may need to be found as the thyroid tissue may not be accessible to surgery

- A skilled surgeon is required: not all veterinarians may feel able to offer this treatment

- Occasionally recurrence can be seen. This can be for one of several reasons listed in order of decreasing frequency:

  - A cat that has had unilateral thyroid disease (only one thyroid lobe affected) may go on to develop disease of the other thyroid lobe in the future. Cats suffering from unilateral hyperthyroidism will develop atrophy (shrinking) of the other thyroid lobe. This makes it difficult to impossible to remove normal thyroid tissue surgically as the risks of causing hypoparathyroidism are greatly increased. Bilateral thyroid disease occurs in around 70% of all hyperthyroid cats making this the most common reason for recurrence of disease

  - A small amount of tissue is left behind during surgery. This tissue can re-grow and lead to recurrence of hyperthyroidism

A typical thyroid mass is being removed from this cat.

  - Multiple abnormal areas of thyroid tissue (for example ectopic tissue as well as both thyroid lobes) are causing the hyperthyroidism. Abnormal thyroid tissue can be very small and difficult to feel or locate at surgery, therefore in these patients it can be difficult to guarantee that all abnormal tissue has been removed. In an ideal world, these patients are best identified prior to surgery using thyroid scintigraphy. Unfortunately scintigraphy facilities are not routinely available in most veterinary practices

- Surgery can be associated with side-effects including those discussed on pages 43-44. Of particular importance is damage to or removal of the parathyroid tissue which causes post-operative hypoparathyroidism. This is discussed in more detail below.

Hypothyroidism (an underactive thyroid) is a rare complication that can occur with surgery. In most cats, with time, ectopic thyroid tissue can develop and take over. Hypothyroidism is discussed in more detail on pages 50-52.

What is post-operative hypoparathyroidism?

Post-operative hypoparathyroidism is the name for the situation which occurs when damage to the parathyroid glands (see above) occurs during thyroid surgery. The frequency of this side-effect varies according to the skill of the surgeon and other factors such as the size of the thyroid and how easy it is to remove. Overall, probably less than 10% of cats having thyroid surgery will suffer from this side-effect.

The parathyroid glands are very sensitive to handling and so can be easily damaged although in many cases, this is temporary. If the parathyroid glands are inadvertently removed then this too will cause hypoparathyroidism. Even in these cases, the hypo parathyroidism is usually temporary since, with time, ectopic tissue can develop and take over.

Hypoparathyroidism causes hypocalcaemia – low blood calcium levels – and this can be fatal.

The risk of hypoparathyroidism occurring is highest when a cat requires a bilateral thyroidectomy (removal of both thyroid glands). For this reason, many veterinarians prefer to 'stage' their thyroidectomies – removing one abnormal thyroid on one day and waiting for a few weeks or months before operating on the second gland. This reduces the risk of hypoparathyroidism as only

This cat has had a thyroidectomy to remove a large thyroid mass. The skin stitches are visible and need to stay in for 7-10 days to allow the wound to heal.

one parathyroid gland is normally required to maintain healthy blood levels of calcium.

Very occasionally hypoparathyroidism can be seen after a unilateral thyroidectomy. In these cases it is thought that handling of both sets of parathyroid glands during tissue manipulation has caused some bruising of the parathyroid glands. Bruising can cause temporary problems with calcium regulation and hence hypoparathyroidism.

If your cat has a thyroidectomy, it is normal for them to be hospitalised for at least 24 hours following surgery so that their progress can be closely monitored. Monitoring usually includes blood tests for calcium levels. Signs of hypocalcaemia often develop within two to three days of surgery and include:

- Loss of appetite
- Weakness
- Anxiety
- Increased sensitivity and over-reaction to touch and sound (hyperaesthesia)
- Twitching and tremors
- Seizures (fits)
- Severely affected cats may lapse into a coma and die if not treated.

Not all cats developing hypoparathyroidism need treatment – as long as the blood calcium levels do not drop too low or too quickly. In those cats that do need treatment, both calcium and vitamin D are usually required. In an emergency situation, calcium may be needed by injection. Vitamin D treatment is important as this helps calcium given by mouth to be absorbed. In many cats, after a few days of treatment, Vitamin D therapy alone is sufficient to stabilise blood calcium levels. For most affected cats, this condition is temporary with the parathyroid glands recovering over a period of days or weeks. During this period, the blood calcium levels are monitored and the dose of calcium and/or Vitamin D altered such that blood calcium levels stay at the bottom of the reference range. In most cats, the dose of treatment is gradually reduced until they no longer require calcium or Vitamin D. Most cats will need some treatment for

a few months, only a very small proportion of cats will need to stay on these medications longer than this.

Radioiodine treatment of hyperthyroidism

Radioiodine (also referred to as ^{131}I) is a form of radiotherapy that is able to treat abnormal thyroid tissue. It is regarded as the 'gold standard' treatment for hyperthyroidism as it is so safe and effective.

Radioiodine contains a very small dose of radioactive iodine. The treatment is given either by oral capsule or by injection and naturally targets the thyroid tissue. Iodine is used by the thyroid gland to produce thyroid hormones. The radioactivity is able to destroy the abnormal thyroid tissue, shrinking the goitre and reducing the amount of thyroid hormones produced.

Radioiodine is regarded as the safest treatment for hyperthyroidism. The dose of radioactivity required is very low and therefore is not damaging to other tissues of the body. There is no risk of damage to the parathyroid glands or any other tissues that can be damaged by surgery. For human health and safety reasons (exposure to radioactivity), some veterinarians prefer to sedate patients if they are injecting the radioiodine.

Hyperthyroid cats receiving antithyroid treatments such as methimazole usually need to stop this treatment one to four weeks before the radioiodine is given – the precise guidelines will vary according to which medication is being used. Cats receiving management with an iodine-restricted food should have this withdrawn two weeks before treatment with radioiodine. Your veterinarian will be able to advise you as to which food is most suitable for your cat during this period and subsequent treatment with radioiodine.

Treatments for high blood pressure and heart disease do not affect the effectiveness of iodine treatment so can be given continuously.

Advantages of radioiodine treatment include:

- No anaesthetic is required
- The treatment is very effective – most reports indicate that about 95% of hyperthyroid cats are cured with a single dose of radioiodine
- All abnormal hyperthyroid tissue is treated – wherever it is located in the cat. This makes radioiodine an excellent treatment for cats with ectopic thyroid disease
- Radioiodine is safe to the parathyroid glands and other tissues of the body, only the thyroid gland is being targeted by this treatment
- It is very rare for the hyperthyroidism to recur following successful treatment
- Side-effects are very rare: hypothyroidism (an underactive thyroid) is common following treatment but usually resolves with time. It is very rare for a cat to remain hypothyroid such that they need treatment for this. In those cats that do need treatment, oral thyroid hormone medication is available and can be used. Hypothyroidism is discussed in more detail later
- Radioiodine is the only treatment that is effective for many cats with thyroid carcinomas. A higher dose of radioiodine is needed in these patients (typically five to ten times the usual dose).

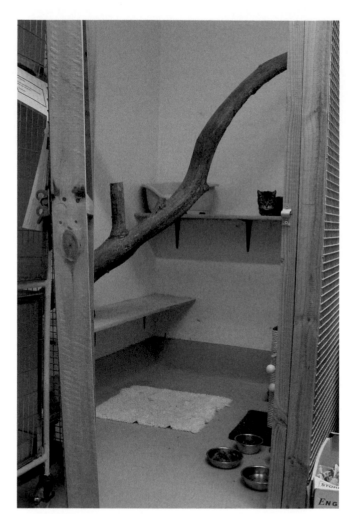

One of the University of Bristol's radioiodine units. Trees, shelves and toys are used to make the environment as stimulating as possible for the cat's hospital stay.

Disadvantages of radioiodine include:

- Since the treatment involves radioactive material, strict human health and safety controls exist in many countries where this treatment is allowed. These regulations, which vary from country to country (and from region to region) require treated cats to be hospitalised in special facilities for a period after their treatment. This is done to limit human exposure to radioactive substances. For example, in the UK, most treated cats must be kept in special hospital facilities for one to five weeks. In some US clinics, this period can be as short as three days although it is more often one to three weeks. In Australia, treated cats typically need to stay in the hospital for five to ten days

- Because of the strict health and safety requirements, available facilities for treatment of hyperthyroid cats with radioiodine are very limited. Waiting lists at individual centres vary according to demand but you should be prepared to find that there may be a delay before treatment can be done. The Appendix contains further information on locating a radioiodine clinic in the UK, North America, Australia and New Zealand. In other regions, the best advice on locating one of these clinics is to ask your own veterinarian or contact the closest University Veterinary School since many of these have radioiodine treatment facilities

- Cats having this treatment need to be in relatively good health since it is not possible to handle them for at least a few days after their treatment. For example, cats requiring daily subcutaneous fluids for chronic kidney disease may not be suitable patients for radioiodine therapy

- In some cats, it can take several months before the full effects of the treatment can be seen. Very occasionally (less than 5-10% cases), a second treatment may be needed

- Although side-effects are very rare with this treatment, occasionally permanent hypothyroidism (an underactive thyroid gland) can be seen. This typically occurs in less than 5% of cats treated with radioiodine and is easily treatable with thyroid hormone supplements as described later.

Other treatments for hyperthyroidism

Other techniques that have been described for hyperthyroid cats include:

- Chemical ablation: this technique involves anaesthesia of the patient before injecting 100% ethanol (an alcohol) into the thyroid tissue, using ultrasound to guide placement of the needle. Published studies have shown that this treatment can be effective, especially in cats with unilateral disease, although multiple treatments may be necessary in some cats. Unfortunately some cats have suffered side effects to adjacent tissues such as the recurrent laryngeal nerve and sympathetic nervous system. So far, this treatment has not been as successful as existing treatment and the reported side effects can be very serious.

- Percutaneous radiofrequency heat ablation: this technique has been studied in a small number of cats. Unfortunately the treatment is only temporarily effective - on average lasting for about four months, the maximum duration reported is 18 months. Side effects can be seen associated with damage to adjacent nerve tissues such as the sympathetic nervous system and recurrent laryngeal nerve. Fortunately in many cases, these side-effects have been temporary. These side effects are explained in more detail on page 44. Repeated treatment was needed in several cats to achieve euthyroidism (reduce the thyroid hormone levels into the normal range).

At present both of these techniques are regarded as experimental procedures, still under evaluation by certain specialist clinicians.

What is hypothyroidism?

Hypothyroidism is the medical term for an underactive thyroid gland which is not producing adequate amounts of thyroid hormones. This can be seen as a congenital condition (present from birth) but is most often seen as a result of treatment for hyperthyroidism.

A recent study showed that cats that developed hypothyroidism following treatment of their hyperthyroidism had a much worse long-term outlook than those cats that remained euthyroid following treatment of their hyperthyroidism. The hypothyroid cats in this study were much more vulnerable to developing renal complications (reduced kidney function). Those cats that did suffer from renal complications had much shorter survival times (lived much shorter lives) compared to the other cats in the study.

Hypothyroidism reduces blood flow to the kidneys and reduces the glomerular filtration rate (a measure of kidney function). This is likely to be an important factor and reason why some cats develop renal complications if they suffer from hypothyroidism.

Given this information, it is important to monitor patients closely following treatment so that hypothyroidism can be diagnosed and treated appropriately. Hypothyroidism is possible with all treatments for hyperthyroidism.

Advice for detection and management of hypothyroidism following treatment of hyperthyroidism varies according to the treatment given:

- Cats receiving management of their hyperthyroidism with antithyroid medication: blood test monitoring of medically treated hyperthyroid cats allows accurate dosing so that if a cat is being over-treated, the dose can be reduced to correct this. Medical treatment should be titrated to maintain euthyroidism – the aim being to suppress total T4 levels to the lower half of the reference range in treated cats. The dose of antithyroid medication should be reduced if total T4 levels fall below the reference range.

- Cats whose hyperthyroidism is managed by feeding an iodine-restricted food may need to stop this food if they develop hypothyroidism although, so far, this has not been reported in any cats receiving this management.

- In cats that have had permanent treatments for their hyperthyroidism, such as iodine or surgery, transient hypothyroidism (lasting up to six months) is common and probably affects up to 30% of patients. In those cats where total T4 levels are persistently low following surgical treatment or radioiodine, a diagnosis of hypothyroidism can be confirmed by performing one or more additional tests such as:

  - Measuring free T4 (pages 18–19): levels are expected to be low in cats suffering from hypothyroidism. However, levels of free T4 can also be suppressed by concurrent illnesses such as chronic kidney disease which may confuse interpretation

  - Measuring TSH levels (pages 19-20): levels are expected to be high in cats suffering from hypothyroidism

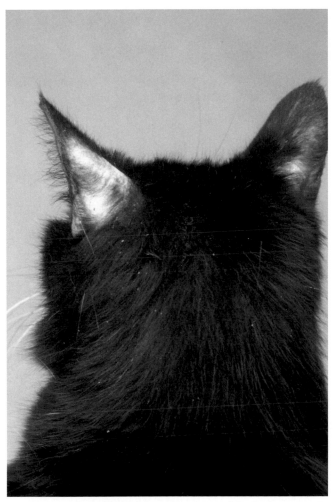

Hypothyroidism (an underactive thyroid) can be seen following treatment of hyperthyroidism. In this patient the hypothyroidism was associated with hair loss over the ears and more dandruff in the coat.

– Performing a TSH stimulation test. The TSH stimulation test involves administering TSH to see whether this will produce an increase in total T4 levels as seen in normal cats (typically at least a two fold increase is seen). In cats suffering from hypothyroidism there is little or no increase in total T4 levels

– Thyroid scintigraphy (pages 25–26): hypothyroid cats show little or no uptake of radioactivity in their thyroid gland when imaged using scintigraphy.

Care needs to be taken not to diagnose hypothyroidism solely on the basis of low total T4 results since these can be suppressed by other illnesses (known as 'sick euthyroid' syndrome). Thyroid hormone supplementation is usually recommended in confirmed cases of post-treatment hypothyroidism. The dose is adjusted according to the patient's progress and their blood thyroid hormone levels. Short-term treatment may be required in some patients but in the majority of affected cats the hypothyroidism eventually completely resolves. Ectopic thyroid tissue is believed to develop and provide sufficient thyroid hormone. Radioiodine therapy for hyperthyroidism carries the highest risk of inducing permanent hypothyroidism but this is probably only seen in less than 5% of cats.

There is one reported case of adult-onset hypothyroidism which was not caused by treatment of hyperthyroidism. In this cat, the illness was caused by an inflammatory disease affecting the thyroid gland (a disease called lymphocytic thyroiditis).

Typical signs of hypothyroidism in an adult cat include:

■ Lethargy and depression

Congenital hypothyroidism is very rare. Typical signs include disproportionate stunting as can be seen in this kitten which was very small with short legs, a short body and a disproportionately large head. (The cat is pictured next to a 400g tin of catfood to give an indication of scale).

- Weight gain
- Coat changes – for example poor hair re-growth (for example if an area of the coat is clipped), hair loss over the ears, dandruff or scurf in the coat
- Constipation
- Heat seeking behaviour – hypothyroid cats may feel cold
- Myxoedema – the face can appear swollen and puffy, especially around the eyes, cheeks and forehead. This can sometimes make the cat look sad so can also be referred to as a 'tragic facial expression'.

Congenital hypothyroidism is very rare although it has been reported in most breeds of cats, including Abyssinian and domestic shorthair (moggies). Typical signs of this illness include:

- Disproportionate stunting – a kitten which is small with very short legs, a short body and a disproportionately large and broad head
- Constipation
- A goitre
- Retained baby teeth (or very delayed replacement of these by the adult teeth)
- Learning difficulties – for example difficult or impossible to litter train
- Lethargy
- Coat changes – for example a thick undercoat
- Heat seeking behaviour – hypothyroid cats may feel cold.

Hypothyroid cats have low blood levels of thyroid hormones which cannot be increased much by administration of TRH or TSH (page 19). Blood levels of TSH are increased in cats with hypothyroidism. Hypothyroid cats often have increased blood levels of cholesterol and a mild anaemia. Affected cats can be treated with thyroid replacement hormone (L-thyroxine) to correct this condition. Congenital cases do not always make a full response to treatment and some care providers elect for euthanasia in cats whose quality of life is considered to be unacceptably poor.

What is the best treatment for my hyperthyroid cat?

As already discussed, all of the treatments available have advantages and disadvantages. The best person to advise you regarding your cat is your own veterinarian since they know you and your cat best. The advantages and disadvantages are summarised in the table below. Often there is not a huge difference in cost between the different treatments. The cost of nutritional and medical treatments are spread over the remaining years of the cat's life rather than required at the start of treatment.

Factor	Medical treatment	Nutritional management	Surgery	Radioiodine
Is it possible to cure the condition with this treatment?	No	No	Yes	Yes
Other than the potential for reduced kidney function which can occur with all treatments for hyperthyroidism, are side-effects possible?	Yes	None reported	Yes	Yes
How common and how serious are the side effects?	< 20% of cats have mild and transient side-effects < 5% of cats have serious side effects	None reported	Typically < 10% of cats suffer side-effects but these can be very serious	< 5% of cats suffer side-effects and these are usually treatable
Is there a risk of permanent hypothyroidism?	No – the dose of treatment can be reduced to resolve this	No – if hypothyroidism is seen the food can be withdrawn	Very rare (< 5%)	Very rare (< 5%)
Is there a risk of recurrence?	Yes	Yes, if the cat eats other foods	Yes	Yes (much less common)
Will my cat need to stay in hospital?	Not usually	No	Yes, usually < 3-5 days	Yes, usually at least 1 week*
Will the treatment be available in my location?	Yes	Available in most countries	Yes	Less common

* the duration of hospitalisation varies enormously according to the location and radiation rules in that area.

Can hyperthyroid cats with chronic kidney disease still receive treatment?

Treatment of hyperthyroid cats with chronic kidney disease is complicated. As discussed earlier (pages 31–32), all treatments for hyperthyroidism have the potential to worsen kidney function. This is because all treatments of hyperthyroidism cause a reduction in blood flow to the kidneys. This has the potential to 'unmask' or reveal kidney disease that was not previously known about and to worsen pre-existing kidney disease.

Treatment of hyperthyroid cats with kidney disease is more complicated since all treatments have the potential to worsen kidney function. Medical management of the hyperthyroidism using antithyroid drugs or nutritional management with an iodine-restricted food are usually recommended since these are reversible. If problems are seen, the dose of antithyroid medication can be reduced (or stopped) or the food can be changed back to normal. Other treatments for kidney disease such as subcutaneous fluid therapy (shown here) can be continued.

Assessment of kidney function is complicated in a cat with hyperthyroidism (see pages 20–21). If a cat is known to have chronic kidney disease before medical treatment is started then your veterinarian may recommend that a lower dose of medication (such as methimazole or carbimazole) is used initially and that the kidney values are monitored closely using blood tests. If any problems are seen, then the dose of treatment can be lowered or even stopped. It can be a delicate balance between treating the thyroid disease and yet not compromising kidney function.

If the kidney disease remains stable on hyperthyroid treatment, and your cat remains well, then more permanent treatments for the hyperthyroidism (such as surgery and radioiodine) can be considered. Treatment for chronic kidney disease is discussed in more detail in another Cat Professional publication 'Caring for a cat with chronic kidney disease'. The recent treatment advances for kidney disease have been very successful in stabilising cats with this condition.

Can hyperthyroid cats with diabetes mellitus still receive treatment?

Treatment of hyperthyroid cats with diabetes mellitus is more complicated. Thyroid hormones cause insulin resistance by interfering with the way insulin (the hormone that regulates blood sugar levels) is able to work. In those cats that are diabetic before they develop hyperthyroidism, the thyroid disease can make medical control of the diabetes more difficult. Often it is necessary to stabilise the hyperthyroidism before the diabetes can, once again, be fully controlled.

Treatment of diabetic hyperthyroid cats is more complicated. Often it is necessary to stabilise the hyperthyroidism before the diabetes can be fully controlled.

A cat whose diabetes was previously well controlled may deteriorate when hyperthyroidism develops. In some cats with both illnesses, a higher dose of insulin might be needed to stabilise blood sugar levels. However, until the thyroid disease has been brought under control, your veterinarian may recommend that a low dose of insulin is used and that your cat's diabetes is monitored closely. This is done to avoid the problem of low blood sugar levels (hypoglycaemia) developing once the thyroid disease comes under control. Hypoglycaemia can be fatal and is much more concerning in the short-term than uncontrolled diabetes mellitus.

In a small number of hyperthyroid cats, insulin resistance caused by this condition can lead to development of diabetes mellitus.

What about cats with thyroid carcinomas?

Thyroid carcinomas are a rare cause of hyperthyroidism (approximately 1 – 2% of patients) but are much more serious. A carcinoma is a type of cancer. The abnormal thyroid tissue not only grows and enlarges causing hyperthyroidism and a goitre but also:

- Can invade healthy tissues adjacent to the thyroid. This often means that the cancer is impossible to remove surgically or that very radical surgery is required (for example removing portions of neck muscle as well as the goitre)
- Can spread to other parts of the body such as the lungs.

Some thyroid carcinomas may be manageable with antithyroid drugs (for example carbimazole or methimazole). Nutritional management with an iodine-restricted food has not been described for thyroid carcinomas. Surgical treatment is not usually advised in these patients since it is generally not possible to remove all of the cancerous tissue, even with radical surgery. The treatment of choice is radioiodine but a much higher dose is required – typically five to ten times the dose needed with 'routine' hyperthyroid cats. This poses some additional problems

Thyroid carcinomas are best treated with a very high dose of radioiodine. This patient had a very successful response to treatment. She was cured of her thyroid disease and lived for many more years with an excellent quality of life.

in terms of human health and safety since the level of radiation is much higher. Only a few locations are able to offer treatment for thyroid carcinomas – in the UK, the University of Bristol and University of Edinburgh are the only places where thyroid carcinomas can be treated (see Useful websites, pages 77–79, for more information).

How can I give my cat the best quality and length of life possible?

For many cats, once stabilised, their care is not difficult, time-consuming or stressful and it is likely that they will enjoy a good quality of life for years.

Regular monitoring and vigilance for development of new problems are essential in ensuring the best care of your cat. It is important to follow your veterinarian's recommendations regarding timing and frequency of check-ups. The precise timing of these varies from cat to cat, according to the treatment regime they are receiving and their progress on this.

A guide to check-ups follows and is sub-divided according to the treatment administered. Cats should be returned for check-ups sooner if you have any concerns. Specific causes for concern include:

- Sudden deterioration or loss of vision
- Loss of appetite which persists for more than 24 hours
- Vomiting more frequently
- Severe lethargy/listlessness

- Scratching and severe itchiness of the skin (especially the head area) in cats receiving antithyroid medication.

Check-ups for hyperthyroid cats receiving medical treatment

Check-ups and monitoring are especially important for cats receiving medical therapy for their hyperthyroidism. Typically these involve:

- History and clinical examination:
  - Aim of these tests: to assess the progress of the patient since starting treatment both looking for evidence suggesting that the hyperthyroidism is now controlled and also for any evidence of side-effects to treatment. For example, a racing heart rate can imply that the disease is still not under control; a healthy weight gain should be seen with successful management of the hyperthyroidism.
  - Frequency of check-up required:
    - It is most common for the first check-up to be timetabled around three weeks after treatment has been started. If the thyroid hormone levels are too high or too low, the treatment dose may need to be changed and a repeat check-up arranged. Repeat check-ups are usually done approximately every three weeks until the thyroid disease is stable and the thyroid hormone levels are within the reference range (known as euthyroidism).
    - For those cats whose hyperthyroidism has been successfully stabilised with antithyroid drugs, check-ups are recommended after a further three, five to six, eight to ten and 20 weeks. After this time, check-ups every three months are recommended for as long as the cat remains

> **Check-ups are especially important for cats receiving antithyroid medication. Although severe side-effects are very rare, they can be fatal if not detected and treated promptly.**

- A check-up every three months ensures that any problem, such as weight loss, is detected promptly and can therefore be addressed quickly.
- Three monthly check–ups maintain good contact with your veterinarian. Good teamwork between you and your veterinarian will lead to the best care and hence, best outcome for your cat.
- In many countries there is a legal requirement to see patients at least every six months if they are receiving prescription medicines such as antithyroid drugs.

on antithyroid medication. Laboratory tests should also be done if there is any concern as a result of the history and/or clinical examination – for example if your veterinarian is suspicious of anaemia (for example if your cat's gums appear very pale) then a haematology profile may be indicated to assess the numbers of red blood cells, platelets and haemoglobin content.

– Why are these check-ups important?

- A veterinary examination is the best way of detecting changes which might not be obvious at home since the care provider is seeing their cat every day. For example, weight loss commonly goes unnoticed by care providers (unless it becomes quite dramatic) as it is impossible to observe a small daily amount of weight loss when you are seeing your cat every day. I have seen many cats that have lost 10-20% of their body weight since the last check-up but whose owners are unaware of any change in their condition (or even think that their cat has gained weight!). Imagine how much weight loss this would be for you and hence how serious a consequence this could be for your cat!

■ Blood pressure measurement (where possible) and eye examination (to look for evidence of high blood pressure) should be done following a diagnosis of hyperthyroidism. Examination of the eyes is something that can easily be done at the general check-ups and therefore can continue to be done whenever the cat comes in for a check-up. Since a proportion of cats develop systemic hypertension after their hyperthyroidism has been treated, continued monitoring is also important following medical stabilisation.

– Aim of these tests: to identify and treat high blood pressure promptly. If left untreated, high blood pressure risks serious consequences such as permanent blindness, kidney damage and death.

– Frequency of check-up required:

- If blood pressure is normal at the initial check then I would advocate a second check within the first two months to ensure that high blood pressure is not being overlooked. If still normal at this point then I would reduce the frequency of blood pressure check-ups to a minimum of two checks per year.

Blood pressure assessment is an important part of the check-up examination. This cat has a leg cuff on in readiness to measure his blood pressure.

- • In those cats needing treatment for systemic hypertension, blood pressure needs to be checked more frequently – especially during the initial period of treatment. Once blood pressure is stable subsequent check-ups can be done less frequently. This is something that I do gradually according to the patient – for example reducing the frequency of blood pressure checks to a minimum of three to four checks per year, even if very stable.

- – Why are such regular check-ups needed in all cats?

- • A proportion of hyperthyroid cats develop systemic hypertension after their hyperthyroidism is treated and it is important to identify and treat these cats. In some of these cats, the high blood pressure is associated with chronic kidney disease. Systemic hypertension is often referred to as the 'silent killer' – it is common to show no outward signs of this condition before severe problems strike. Blood pressure checks ensure that high blood pressure is identified quickly helping to prevent development of consequences associated with this condition.

- ■ Repeat laboratory tests: haematology, serum biochemistry, urinalysis and total thyroxine (tT4)

  - – Aim of these tests:

  - • To check whether the thyroid disease is under control (i.e. whether or not the thyroid hormone levels are within the reference range), to assess whether there are any concurrent illnesses and to look for side-effects associated with the treatment (e.g. changes to the haematology). Most side-effects are seen within the first few months of therapy and laboratory tests are especially important during this period.

  - – Frequency of check-up required:

> **Severe side-effects of antithyroid medication are very rare but can be fatal. Monitoring is essential to detect side-effects – if treated promptly, most affected cats make a full recovery.**

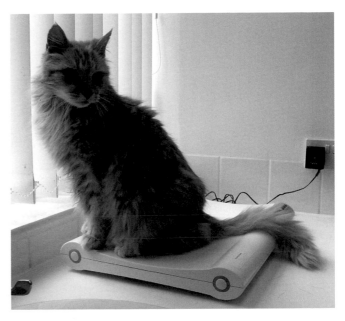

Weight checks are very important – success of treatment can be partly assessed by monitoring the cat's bodyweight.

- For cats whose hyperthyroidism is still not fully controlled (thyroid hormone levels still too high), repeat tT4 assessment is usually recommended two to three weeks after any treatment dose change until euthyroidism is achieved. At these checks it is desirable, where possible, to include additional laboratory tests to check kidney function and look for potential side-effects to treatment.

- For those cats whose hyperthyroidism has been successfully stabilised with antithyroid drugs, check-ups are recommended after a further three, five to six, eight to ten and 20 weeks. After this time, check-ups every three months are recommended for as long as the cat remains on antithyroid medication. As discussed earlier, laboratory tests should also be done if there is any specific concern as a result of the history and/or clinical examination such as anaemia or weight loss.

  – Why are these check-ups important?

- Laboratory tests are important to ensure that treatment is successful and to check for evidence of any side-effects. For example, it is important to look for worsening of kidney function that may necessitate a reduction in the dose of antithyroid medication. In addition, as discussed on page 34, laboratory tests are needed to look for evidence of severe side-effects associated with antithyroid treatment. Although severe side-effects are very rare, these can be fatal in some cats. Prompt treatment provides the best chance of a successful outcome.

Check-ups for hyperthyroid cats that are being managed with an iodine-restricted food

■ History and clinical examination:

  – Aim of these tests: to assess the progress of the patient since starting treatment both looking for evidence suggesting

Dilation of the pupils (i) is one potential indication of blindness associated with high blood pressure as in this case. When a light is shone into the cat's eyes (ii), the pupils remain large and the retina can be seen (both of these findings are abnormal). Small areas of bleeding can also be seen in the cat's left eye – another consequence of her high blood pressure. Unfortunately the blindness was permanent in this cat.

that the hyperthyroidism is now controlled and also for any evidence of side-effects to treatment. For example, loss of appetite and increased thirst could indicate that the cat is suffering from renal complications whereas a healthy weight gain may indicate successful control of the hyperthyroidism.

– Frequency of check-up required:

• Check-ups are recommended once the cat has been eating the food exclusively for 4, 8 and 12 weeks. More frequent check-ups may be justified in cats where there are concerns of renal complications. Many cats will be euthyroid at their first check-up although some may take as long as 12 weeks to respond fully to the food.

• For those cats whose hyperthyroidism has been successfully stabilised with an iodine-restricted food, three monthly check-ups are recommended. Laboratory tests should be done if there are any concerns as a result of the history and/or physical examination – for example if your cat has lost weight then blood tests may be indicated to check total T4 levels and look for other causes of weight loss

– Why are these check-ups important?

• A veterinary examination is the best way of detecting changes which might not be obvious at home since the care provider is seeing their cat every day. For example, weight loss commonly goes unnoticed by care providers as it is impossible to observe a small daily amount of weight loss when you are seeing your cat every day.

• A check-up every three months ensures that any problem, such as weight loss, is detected promptly and can therefore be addressed quickly.

- Three monthly check–ups maintain good contact with your veterinarian. Good teamwork between you and your veterinarian will lead to the best care and hence, best outcome for your cat.

■ Blood pressure measurement (where possible) and eye examination (to look for evidence of high blood pressure) should be done following a diagnosis of hyperthyroidism. Examination of the eyes is something that can easily be done at the general check-ups and therefore can continue to be done whenever the cat comes in for a check-up. Since a proportion of cats develop systemic hypertension *after* their hyperthyroidism has been treated, continued monitoring is also important following stabilisation with an iodine-restricted food.

  - Aim of these tests: to identify and treat high blood pressure promptly. If left untreated, high blood pressure risks serious consequences such as permanent blindness, kidney damage and death.

  - Frequency of check-up required:

    • If blood pressure is normal at the initial check then I would advocate a second check within the first two months to ensure that high blood pressure is not being overlooked. If still normal at this point then I would reduce the frequency of blood pressure check-ups to a minimum of two checks per year.

    • In those cats needing treatment for systemic hypertension, blood pressure needs to be checked more frequently – especially during the initial period of treatment. Once blood pressure is stable subsequent check-ups can be done less frequently. This is something that I do gradually according to the patient – for example reducing the frequency of blood pressure checks to a minimum of three to four checks per year, even if very stable.

An increased thirst can be present in cats with uncontrolled hyperthyroidism and other conditions including, most commonly, chronic kidney disease.

  - Why are such regular check-ups needed in all cats? A proportion of hyperthyroid cats develop systemic hypertension after their hyperthyroidism is treated and it is important to identify and treat these cats. In some of these cats, the high blood pressure is associated with chronic kidney disease. Systemic hypertension is often referred to as the 'silent killer' – it is common to show no outward signs of this condition before severe problems strike. Blood pressure checks ensure that high blood pressure is identified quickly helping to prevent development of consequences associated with this condition.

■ Repeat laboratory tests: haematology, serum biochemistry, urinalysis and total thyroxine (tT4)

- Aim of these tests:
  - To check whether the thyroid disease is under control (i.e. whether or not the thyroid hormone levels are within the reference range), to assess whether there are any concurrent illnesses and to look for side-effects associated with the treatment (e.g. hypothyroidism, renal complications). Most side-effects are seen within the first few months of therapy and laboratory tests are especially important during this period.

- Frequency of check-up required:
  - For cats whose hyperthyroidism is still not fully controlled (thyroid hormone levels still too high), repeat tT4 assessment is usually recommended every four weeks until euthyroidism is achieved. Most cats will be euthyroid within 12 weeks of exclusively eating the iodine-restricted food. At these checks it is desirable, where possible, to include additional laboratory tests to check kidney function.
  - For those cats whose hyperthyroidism has been successfully stabilised with an iodine-restricted food, check-ups are recommended every six months. As discussed earlier, laboratory tests should also be done if there is any specific concern as a result of the history and/or clinical examination such as weight loss.

- Why are these check-ups important?
  - Laboratory tests are important to ensure that treatment is successful and to check for evidence of any side-effects. For example, it is important to look for worsening of kidney function that may necessitate a change in food

Check-ups for hyperthyroid cats that have had surgical treatment or radioiodine

Check-ups are still very important in these cats. Typically these involve:

- History and clinical examination:
  - Aim of these tests: to assess the progress of the patient since treatment was given both looking for evidence suggesting that the hyperthyroidism is now controlled and also for any evidence of side-effects related to the treatment. For example, hair loss over the ears can be an indication of hypothyroidism; an increased thirst may be an indication of chronic kidney disease.

  - Frequency of check-up required:
    - Cats that have had surgical treatment will usually be reassessed a few days after their surgery so that their surgical wound can be checked for any swelling or other problems. If stitches have been placed in the skin, these will normally need to stay in for 7 - 10 days.
    - Cats that have suffered from post-operative hypoparathyroidism need frequent assessments (for example weekly) and careful management until their hypoparathyroidism has resolved. Dosages of calcium and vitamin D need to be carefully titrated in these cats to ensure that they are receiving the correct treatment.
    - Cats that have had radioiodine treatment will usually have check-ups at around one and three months following their treatment.

- In the long-term, cats that have had surgical or radioiodine treatment benefit from check-ups every three to six months. The main reason for these check-ups is to look for evidence of recurrence of hyperthyroidism and emergence of new problems such as kidney disease. A history and clinical examination helps to pick up clues of these such as weight loss.

– Why are these check-ups important?

- A veterinary examination is the best way of detecting changes which might not be obvious at home since the care provider is seeing their cat every day. For example, weight loss commonly goes unnoticed by care providers (unless it becomes quite dramatic) as it is impossible to observe a small daily amount of weight loss when you are seeing your cat every day. A check-up every three to six months ensures that any problem, such as weight loss, is detected promptly and can therefore be addressed quickly.

- Three to six monthly check–ups maintain good contact with your veterinarian. Good teamwork between you and your veterinarian will lead to the best care and hence, best outcome for your cat.

■ Blood pressure measurement (where possible) and eye examination (to look for evidence of high blood pressure) should be done following a diagnosis of hyperthyroidism. Examination of the eyes is something that can easily be done at the general check-ups and therefore can continue to be done whenever the cat comes in for a check-up. Since a proportion of cats develop systemic hypertension after their hyperthyroidism has been treated, continued monitoring is also important following radioiodine and thyroid surgery.

– Aim of these tests: to identify and treat high blood pressure promptly. If left untreated, high blood pressure risks serious consequences such as permanent blindness, kidney damage and death.

– Frequency of check-up required:

- If blood pressure is normal at the initial check then I would advocate a second check within the first two months to ensure that high blood pressure is not being overlooked. If still normal at this point then I would reduce the frequency of blood pressure check-ups to a minimum of two checks per year.

- In those cats needing treatment for systemic hypertension, blood pressure needs to be checked more frequently – especially during the initial period of treatment. Once blood pressure is stable subsequent check-ups can be done less frequently. This is something that I do gradually according to the patient – for example reducing the frequency of blood pressure checks to a minimum of three to four checks per year, even if very stable.

– Why are such regular check-ups needed in all cats?

- A proportion of hyperthyroid cats develop systemic hypertension after their hyperthyroidism is treated and it is important to identify and treat these cats. In some of these cats, the high blood pressure is associated with chronic kidney disease. Systemic hypertension is often referred to as the 'silent killer' – it is common to show no outward signs of this condition before severe problems strike. Blood pressure checks ensure that high blood pressure is identified quickly helping to prevent development of consequences associated with this condition.

Sudden blindness, often associated with dramatic dilatation of the pupils (the black slit in the centre of the eye becomes very large and round, as in this cat), is a veterinary emergency. Systemic hypertension is the most common cause of this.

■ Repeat laboratory tests: haematology, serum biochemistry, urinalysis and total thyroxine (tT4)

  – Aim of these tests:

■ To check whether the thyroid disease has recurred (i.e. whether or not the thyroid hormone levels are within the reference range), to assess whether there are any concurrent illnesses and to look for side-effects associated with the treatment (such as worsened kidney function).

  – Frequency of check-up required:

    • Check-ups are recommended at one and three months after surgery or radioiodine. Very occasionally, some hyperthyroid cats treated with radioiodine may take longer

than three months to become euthyroid. Further testing (eg TSH testing, TRH stimulation test) may be needed to diagnose post-treatment hypothyroidism in some patients

    • After this period, if all remains well, check-ups are recommended every 6 –12 months. Laboratory tests should also be done if there is any concern as a result of the history and/or clinical examination – for example if your cat has lost weight, a thyroid hormone test may be indicated to assess whether the hyperthyroidism has recurred.

  – Why are these check-ups important?

    • 'Unmasking' of kidney disease or worsening of existing kidney disease can occur following treatment for hyperthyroidism. It is important to identify this as soon as possible so that appropriate treatment can be given.

    • It is important to confirm that the surgical or radioiodine treatment has been successful in treating the hyperthyroidism. In some cats, radioiodine can take several months to be fully effective.

    • Hyperthyroidism can recur following surgical and radioiodine treatment. Laboratory tests help to identify any recurrence quickly so that this can be treated.

Are routine vaccinations and worming still needed in cats with hyperthyroidism?

Cats with stable and well managed hyperthyroidism still benefit from routine preventative health care such as vaccination. All illnesses can reduce a cat's ability to fight infections so they will be more vulnerable to severe illness if they contract an infection. Visits to a veterinary practice can be stressful (which can lower immunity) and risk contact with infectious agents.

As always, follow your veterinarian's advice on what is most appropriate for your cat.

What is the prognosis (long-term outlook) for cats with hyperthyroidism?

Overall, most hyperthyroid cats live for between two and five years following diagnosis of this condition. The best prognosis is reported in those cats treated with radioiodine. Cats that are diagnosed with hyperthyroidism at a younger age are expected to live for longer than cats that are very old at the time of diagnosis. Well controlled thyroid disease is not expected to shorten life expectancy.

The prognosis varies quite markedly in affected cats and this is related to:

- Whether the cat has other concurrent illnesses which may have a life-shortening effect. A common example would be chronic kidney disease. Cats with severe concurrent kidney disease have a reduced lifespan compared to otherwise healthy hyperthyroid cats

- Whether the cat has severe complications associated with their thyroid disease. Although these usually improve with treatment of the thyroid condition, some can still be difficult to fully control. One example would be a cat suffering from severe heart disease – often heart medications are needed for the rest of the cat's life, even when the thyroid disease has been successfully treated.

Anna

Anna was one of the first patients I treated with radioiodine when I was working at the University of Bristol. She was referred with a typical history of hyperthyroidism – she had lost weight, had intermittent diarrhoea, was very hyperactive and irritable and had an insatiable appetite. She was eating several tins of catfood every day and still losing weight. Her poor owner had taken to sleeping downstairs so that she could feed Anna more frequently during the night!

Anna's hyperthyroidism was very advanced and this made her almost impossible to examine – she was very feisty! Her hyperthyroidism had caused a large goitre, a very rapid heart rate, she was very thin and her levels of tT4 were extremely high (190 nmol/l when the reference range is 20 – 45 nmol/l). She had slightly increased levels of liver enzymes but the remainder of her blood and urine tests were fine. Anna had an enlarged heart as a result of her hyperthyroidism but she was not suffering from congestive heart failure. I recommended radioiodine treatment for Anna – she had been a difficult cat to give antithyroid medications to, iodine-restricted foods for management of hyperthyroidism were not available and her owner was keen for her to have the best treatment possible. She had a single subcutaneous (under the skin) injection of iodine and stayed in our hospital for a few weeks whilst she was considered 'radioactive'. At the end of her hospitalisation period, we checked Anna's tT4 levels and found that her condition had been cured (her tT4 levels were now 23 nmol/l, within the reference range). She'd also gained a healthy amount of weight and was looking much happier.

Anna's owner sent me several pictures of Anna, before and after her treatment. In the pre-treatment picture you can appreciate how thin and anxious she looks. Just a few months later, after her radioiodine treatment, she looks a completely different cat. Not only has she gained weight, but she also has a very relaxed expression. Her owner reported that Anna was 'really very healthy and content' and she was delighted that she had improved so much. Anna continued to do very well and is a great example of how well this treatment can work.

Anna before (left) and a few months after (right) treatment with radioiodine. Before treatment she was painfully thin and very anxious. The second photo shows a contented Anna who is now a healthy weight.

The Wilkinson hyperthyroid cats (written by their owner, Kathy)

I know quite a bit about hyperthyroidism as a result of having had seven cats diagnosed with this condition over the last ten years. No two cats have been the same in the clinical signs they've shown or in their response to treatment. Several of our cats have only been diagnosed because of a routine check – not all of them have had really obvious clinical signs. They've all been treated using antithyroid medications with thyroid surgery also done in most of the cats. In some of the cats, surgery has not been appropriate and these cats have remained on lifelong antithyroid treatment. My knowledge of this disease has helped us to diagnose the condition earlier and I hope that this has led to a better treatment outcome for my cats.

Our first cat to be diagnosed was Tiffany, a 13 year old tabby and white shorthair moggy (domestic short hair). She started to hide away under the bed, which wasn't like her at all, and seemed very weak and depressed. Our vet said that her heart was beating so fast it was difficult to count. Blood tests confirmed that she was hyperthyroid, with 'apathetic' disease. This is one of the more unusual presentations of this condition and is usually seen in cats with severe heart disease.

Tiffany was an absolute nightmare to give tablets to – she got so distressed with our attempts that it was easier for us to go to the surgery every day for three weeks and ask them to medicate her! Fortunately her operation went well and she came home three days later. Although she had a slow recovery from her surgery, she gradually improved and went back to her old self. Unfortunately about seven months later she developed another problem from which she passed away.

L to R: Tiffany and Tabitha.

Having learnt a lot about hyperthyroidism through Tiffany and her illness, we soon realised that her litter sister, Tabitha, also 13 years old and tabby and white, was showing what seemed to be the textbook signs. She'd lost weight in spite of having an excellent appetite and had also become very irritable. Our vets confirmed that she too was hyperthyroid. Luckily she was much better at taking pills – especially if we hid them in a piece of meat – so we stabilised her at home before she had thyroid surgery. All went well and she made great progress following her operation. Unfortunately, about two years later, her hyperthyroidism recurred and she developed other problems. She now has systemic hypertension (and therefore can't see very well) and chronic kidney disease which means that she is not a good candidate for further surgery. We're treating her hyperthyroidism and systemic hypertension with medication and keeping a close eye on her. Tabitha was also diagnosed as being diabetic not long after her initial surgery, but within about six months she self-cured – not many cats do that I am told, but she's my miracle old girl!

L to R: Henry, Teddy, Nimrod.

About a year after Tiffany and Tabitha were diagnosed, I became suspicious of signs that two of my 14 year old moggies (Henry and Teddy) were showing, and they too had blood tests for hyperthyroidism. Both cats seemed to be losing weight in spite of a very good appetite. Teddy and Henry are moggy brothers that are not related to Tiffany and Tabitha but are a similar age. Henry's T4 was within normal limits, but he was found to have a heart problem so needed treatment for this. He continued to have regular blood tests to check for hyperthyroidism, and started antithyroid medication when the levels increased. In spite of increasing doses of antithyroid drugs, his T4 levels increased and were affecting his heart. We made a decision for him to have thyroid surgery fairly quickly as he seemed to be deteriorating very rapidly. The operation went very well, and he continued to have regular blood tests and heart scans.

Henry did very well for about 18 months after his surgery but then we found that his hyperthyroidism was recurring. He had a second thyroidectomy, aged 17, as we did not want him to deteriorate and not be well enough for surgery. Unfortunately, although Henry recovered well from his thyroid surgery and his heart and kidneys remained in good condition, he developed another problem which was the cause of his death in March 2009.

Henry's brother Teddy also developed hyperthyroidism when he was 14 years old. However, he was found to have kidney problems and treating both this and the hyperthyroidism proved very difficult. It was like walking a knife's edge coping with the kidney problems and hyperthyroidism. We were able to keep him stable on antithyroid medication for about 18 months but sadly his quality of life deteriorated and eventually we asked our vet to put him to sleep.

At the beginning of 2008 Nimrod, a 12 year old male Tonkinese of mine was showing signs that I recognised from the other cats – including weight loss, vomiting and diarrhoea. He proved a difficult patient to diagnose as his total T4 was within the normal range. In spite of this, I was convinced that he was hyperthyroid and managed to persuade my vet to run a free-T4 test. I was very pleased as this confirmed my diagnosis! Nimrod had a reaction to the antithyroid treatment he was prescribed – he developed a very itchy head and neck. Fortunately we managed to stabilise him on a different treatment and he then had a thyroidectomy. His thyroid surgery was successful and his blood results are still all fine although we are monitoring him closely.

JD, one of my Mum's cats who I look after, was the next cat to develop this condition. At the time, she was nine and was found to have an enlarged thyroid gland on a routine check by our vet. She too was stabilised medically before having surgery. This was successful, and on her first three month check her hormone levels were fine. However at the next three month check they were high, so we decided to stabilise her medically before having a second thyroidectomy. She's made an excellent recovery and her blood test results continue to be fine at the moment.

Finally, another of my Tonkinese (Bruno, a half brother to Nimrod) developed hyperthyroidism. He was being closely monitored for early kidney disease which had been diagnosed six months previously. A routine blood test to check his kidney function showed that he was also hyperthyroid. It came as a big shock to us as there had been no suggestion that he might be suffering from hyperthyroidism. We managed to stabilise his thyroid disease without causing any problems to his kidneys and he was able to have surgery later in the year. After his surgery, he developed an unusual complication called Horner's syndrome. This occurs when there is damage to the nerves that supply the eyes (the sympathetic nervous system). Thankfully he gradually improved and within a few weeks you couldn't tell that he had had a 'funny' eye. His kidneys have remained fine and he continues to have regular checks for these as well as for his thyroid.

I think the worse part of coping with hyperthyroidism in cats is giving the medication. It may be difficult enough to get a ten day course of antibiotics into a cat, but to face a future of once or twice daily medication is really difficult. The cost of the surgery is initially off-putting, especially when there are still regular blood checks to be done afterwards, but at least most of my cats have not needed long-term medication to keep their hyperthyroidism under control.

My choice to let my hyperthyroid cats have surgery was partly because of the difficulties associated with medicating some of my cats but also because I wanted to cure the hyperthyroidism, if at all possible. My local practice has an excellent vet who does all of the thyroid operations and this helped to reassure me about the procedure.

I would have liked to have had radioactive iodine (radioiodine) treatment for my cats but unfortunately there are often waiting lists for treatment and UK regulations mean that treated cats are usually away from home for several weeks which has put me off. I would be happier if two of my cats could go together – the Tonkinese in particular are cats that get very lonely if they don't have company. When I've discussed hyperthyroidism with US cat friends, I've found that radioactive iodine is very popular and that a typical hospitalisation period is much shorter (usually 10-14 days).

My biggest concern, however, is worrying about why I have had so many hyperthyroid cats. I would love to know the answer so that I can avoid my younger cats suffering from this condition. I have read about all sorts of factors that have been studied as possible causes of hyperthyroidism but I am still frustrated that more is not known.

Bruno.

Lucy

Lucy is a beautiful 14 year old long haired cat who lives with her owner Lynda. Lynda took Lucy to be checked by her veterinarian since she was concerned about weight loss and some changes in Lucy's behaviour. Lucy was grooming more and seemed anxious, on edge, and unhappy being handled which was very unlike her. Although she wasn't eating more than usual, Lynda felt that she was much less fussy about her food. Lucy's vet found a rapid heart rate, a gallop rhythm and some loss of condition but otherwise everything looked fine. Blood tests confirmed hyperthyroidism. Lucy's vet discussed initial management of the hyperthyroidism using oral antithyroid medication but this was going to be very difficult for Lynda since Lucy is a tricky cat to pill and Lynda has a disability giving her severe mobility problems. Fortunately, Lynda's vet had attended a lecture given by Dr Sarah Caney during the same week at which time the use of a new iodine-restricted food was mentioned as a possible management option. At this time, only limited supplies of this food were available but Dr Caney was able to provide some for Lynda to try with Lucy. Lucy is a good candidate for this management since she is an indoor-only cat living on her own so it is not difficult to ensure that she only eats one type of food.

Lucy took to the new food immediately and within a week was only eating the iodine-restricted food. At her check-up a month later, she had gained weight, her coat condition had improved and she had a normal heart rate and rhythm. Lynda reported that Lucy was more relaxed and content. Lucy's blood tests also improved – her tT4 levels were within the reference range within 8 weeks of management. Lucy has continued to do well, remaining in excellent condition and very happy in herself. She has now been on her iodine-restricted food for more than ten months.

Lynda says: 'Lucy has now entered her 15th year and I have to say this is the happiest she has been in years all thanks to the iodine-restricted food. Options discussed once the diagnosis of hyperthyroidism was made were tablets, radioactive iodine or an iodine-restricted food. Lucy was a very highly strung cat which was normal for her; I didn't want to increase her stress levels so I knew that the first two options were out as they would affect Lucy's quality of life. I jumped at the chance of the iodine-restricted food because I felt that it was the best option for Lucy and that she wouldn't be put under any undue stress. I was really happy at Lucy's check-up that everything was going the right way. She still loves the food and I can say it is the best thing that could have happened to her, it has improved the quality of her life.'

Lucy

A good relationship with your veterinarian is vital to the care and wellbeing of your cat with hyperthyroidism. It is important therefore that you feel able to discuss all of your concerns openly. Your veterinarian is in the best position to advise you regarding specific questions on treatment and prognosis. You should feel able to ask your veterinarian any questions and they should be able to explain things to you clearly in a way you can understand.

A good relationship with your vet is vital to the care and wellbeing of your cat with hyperthyroidism.

If you feel that the relationship you have with your veterinarian is not answering your concerns then you can ask to see another veterinarian within the practice, or look for another practice. Do not feel uncomfortable if you want to do this – your veterinarian should not mind and it is within your rights to choose the veterinarian you feel is best able to look after your cat. It is always worthwhile asking if there is anyone in the practice who is particularly interested in cat medicine. The UK cat charity, the Feline Advisory Bureau, has a list of UK (and some overseas) vet practices that are members of the charity (see www.fabcats.org/owners/choosing_a_vet/practice_members1.php). Belonging to this charity is a good indication of enthusiasm and knowledge in feline medicine. A number of feline-only practices also exist and you may be fortunate in finding one of these in your area. Cat owners can also consult the American Association of Feline Practitioners website for information on finding a cat-friendly veterinarian in the US and other countries (see www.catvets.com/findadoctor/findadoctor.aspx).

Veterinarians specialising in feline medicine can be contacted by your veterinarian for further advice, if needed, or referral to a specialist can be arranged.

In order for your veterinarian to be able to provide the level of care you are looking for with your cat, they will need to understand things from your perspective. For example:

- Will you be able to medicate your cat at home or is this out of the question (for example because your cat is very feisty or because you have severe arthritis in your fingers)? Will giving some treatments be possible (e.g. nutritional management) but others not possible (e.g. tablets)?

- What are your expectations for your cat? For example, would you prefer minimum intervention accepting a potentially shorter time with your cat or are you keen for your cat to have every possible treatment?

- Are there any treatments which you object to being used in your cat?

- Are finances limited in which case certain treatments may be too expensive? Your veterinarian will be able to advise you on the likely cost of treating your cat.

Once both of you know what your expectations are then it should be possible to jointly work out a treatment plan that is appropriate for your cat.

Misty, a hyperthyroid cat stabilised with oral antithyroid medication

The information in this section is particularly relevant to owners of cats suffering from severe disease such as hyperthyroidism which is difficult to treat because of its severity or presence of concurrent illnesses such as chronic kidney disease.

Knowing when to say 'goodbye'

How long has my cat got before he/she dies or needs to be put to sleep (euthanased)?

This is an impossible question for anyone to answer as it varies enormously from cat to cat. Most cats can live a normal quality of life for many years after a diagnosis of hyperthyroidism has been made. Sadly some die or need to be put to sleep (euthanased). This may be because of the severity of their disease or because they have other concurrent problems which are affecting them. Your veterinarian is in the best position to advise on your own cat and its likely prognosis.

Will I know when it's time to say goodbye to my cat and let him/her go?

It is very rare for a sick cat to die painlessly in their sleep – much though most care providers would wish this to happen. Death tends to be a slow and distressing process and it is far kinder to intervene and ask a veterinarian to put your cat to sleep (euthanase it) when the time has come than let your cat suffer a prolonged and possibly painful death. It is therefore a sad inevitability that one day you are likely to have to decide that your cat needs putting to sleep. For many care providers the thought of making this decision is painful and worrying. Most care providers feel that their cat should be put to sleep once their quality of life has deteriorated and there is no veterinary treat-ment that can help to improve this. Your veterinarian should be able to support and guide you in making this decision – if you are at all worried then consult them for advice.

Quality of life is not easy to judge but guidelines include:

- Behaviour:

a) Is your cat still behaving in its normal way – following its usual routines and activities (e.g. spending the same amount of time grooming)? Is your cat interacting with you as normal?

b) OR, has your cat become withdrawn and quiet, not interested in going outside (if normally allowed out) or in interacting with you and other animals in the home?

- Appetite:

a) Is your cat still interested in food?

b) OR, has their appetite disappeared and getting them to eat has become a struggle?

- Toileting behaviour:

a) Is your cat still passing urine and faeces in the litter tray (or outside in the garden) as is normal for them?

b) OR, has your cat started to pass urine and faeces in other places (such as on their bed or on your carpets and flooring)?

- Vocalisation:

a) Is your cat as chatty as normal?

b) OR, has there been a change in the amount of vocalisation (increase or decrease) or the sound that your cat makes when miaowing?

- Pain or distress:

a) Does your cat seem happy and comfortable?

b) OR, have you seen any sign of pain or discomfort – for example signs of fear or aggression when being handled or sitting in the same place for hours with a glazed expression?

- Signs of illness:

a) Is your cat free of signs of illness?

b) OR, is it suffering from signs of illness such as vomiting, weight loss or constipation?

If you answer b) to any of the above questions then you should consult your vet for advice on whether there are any treatments that can help your cat to regain its quality of life. If there are, you need to consider whether to give these treatments a try before making any final decisions.

What does euthanasia involve?

For most veterinary surgeons, euthanasia involves giving an over-dose injection of a barbiturate anaesthetic agent intravenously, usually into a vein in the front leg. Once the injection is started, the cat will lose consciousness within a few seconds and the heart should stop within a few minutes. Occasionally, the veins of the front leg can be very fragile and difficult to access so alternative injection sites need to be used – these include the kidneys and the liver. In any case, the process should be quick and painless.

Although the majority of cats are put to sleep at a veterinary practice, most vets will be happy to come to an owner's home to do this, if desired.

What happens to my cat's body after they die or are euthanased (put to sleep)?

In general the options will be:

- Burying your cat's body at home.
- Asking your vet to arrange cremation of your cat's body. If desired, you can ask for an individual cremation to be performed and for the ashes to be returned to you.

Your vet will be able to discuss these options with you. It is worthwhile considering how you would like your cat to be put to sleep (should the need arise) and what you would like to happen to their body while your cat is still well. This will save you the added distress of these decisions when your cat dies.

How to cope with losing your cat

Is there support available for me in my grief?
Losing a beloved cat is always going to be a traumatic and distressing experience and you are likely to go through several acknowledged stages of grief. These include denial, anger, guilt, hopelessness/depression and finally acceptance. Most people experience at least two of these. Carers of cats with terminal

illnesses may start to go through this process as soon as the diagnosis is made. Where this is the case, a further stage of grief – 'bargaining' – may also be experienced where a care provider is keen for their cat to live to a certain point (for example, please let them live through Christmas so we can have this time together).

Hopefully you will have friends and family that will be able to provide some support to you throughout this period. If you don't, then consider talking to the veterinarians or nurses at your veterinary practice, your doctor or a priest – all of whom should be able to offer support. There may be local support groups available (your veterinary practice should know about these) and there is also a UK helpline available for dedicated pet bereavement counselling, the Pet Bereavement Support Service

(PBSS): 0800 096 6606 open from 8.30am to 8.30pm daily. All calls are free and confidential. The PBSS also offers an e-mail support service: pbssmail@bluecross.org.uk

More information on this service is available on: www.bluecross.org.uk/2083/pet-bereavement-support-service.html

What about my other cat/s – are they likely to grieve?

Yes this is possible. As with people, cats can show grief at the loss of a companion. The behaviour of a cat following the loss of a house-mate is very variable and unpredictable. Some cats seem completely unaffected by the loss, some appear happier once they are on their own whilst others may show signs of grief such as sleeping less, not eating, appearing to look for their lost companion and vocalising more or losing all interest in life.

This process can affect cats (and other animals) for up to a year following their loss. In most cases, signs of grief will disappear within six months. You can help affected cats in the following ways:

- Keep routines in the home the same
- If your cat has lost its appetite then try hand-feeding food that has been slightly warmed (to just below body temperature). Consult your veterinarian if your cat has not eaten for three or more days. A complete loss of appetite can cause a potentially fatal liver disease called hepatic lipidosis
- Provide social interaction for your cat by spending more time with them, grooming them, talking to them and playing with them. Try to keep the interaction low key and avoid intense handling and cuddling which could appear restrictive from a feline point of view
- Don't immediately get a new cat. Although some cats will crave the company of a new companion, the majority of cats will be more upset and distressed if a new cat is introduced too soon. Many cats prefer to be in single cat households and it is impossible to predict what they will feel about a newcomer. So, if your cat seems happy after the loss of a house-mate I would not recommend getting another cat. If, on the other hand, you are keen to expand the home or feel that your cat is 'lonely' then I would advise waiting for at least a couple of months before considering introducing a new cat. If a new cat does move in

it will need to bring with it a new supply of resources (food, water, resting places and toileting areas) which are placed in separate locations in the household from those resources that are currently being used by the resident cat.

More information on feline bereavement is available on the FAB website: www.fabcats.org/owners/euthanasia/bereavement.html. The FAB also has advice on introducing a new cat which could be helpful once a decision has been made to get another cat: www.fabcats.org/behaviour/introducing/info.html

Useful websites

Several websites have been mentioned in this publication and you might find these interesting to look at:

General cat advice
The Feline Advisory Bureau (FAB)
www.fabcats.org
The Blue Cross
www.bluecross.org.uk/
Cats Protection
www.cats.org.uk/
The Royal Society for the Prevention of Cruelty to Animals
www.rspca.org.uk/
The Cat Group
www.fabcats.org/cat_group/index.html
American Association of Feline Practitioners
www.catvets.com/

Choosing a veterinary practice
The Feline Advisory Bureau
www.fabcats.org/owners/choosing_a_vet/practice_members1.php
American Association of Feline Practitioners (AAFP)
www.catvets.com/findadoctor/findadoctor.aspx

General information on hyperthyroidism
FAB factsheet
www.fabcats.org/owners/hyperthyroidism/index.php

AAFP factsheet
www.catvets.com/healthtopics/medical%5Fconditions/?Id=212

Winn Feline Health
www.winnfelinehealth.org/health/hyperthyroidism.html

Information from Washington State University
www.vetmed.wsu.edu/ClientED/hyperthyroidism.aspx

Information from Dechra Veterinary Products
www.hyperthyroidcat.co.uk/

Information from Pet Education
www.peteducation.com/article.cfm?c=1+2130&aid=218

Information from Dr Mark Peterson and Hypurrcat
www.hypurrcat.com/index2.html

Video tutorial on how to give a pill or capsule to a cat
www.vetprofessionals.com/catprofessional/free_downloads.html

Bereavement support
Information from The Blue Cross
www.bluecross.org.uk/2083/pet-bereavement-support-service.html

Information from the Feline Advisory Bureau
www.fabcats.org/owners/euthanasia/bereavement.html

Introducing a new cat to the home
Information from the Feline Advisory Bureau
www.fabcats.org/behaviour/introducing/info.html

The Indoor cat initiative – making your home environment as stimulating as possible for your cat
http://indoorpet.osu.edu/

Information on legal prescription of veterinary drugs in the UK

www.noahcompendium.co.uk/Compendium/Overview/-45043.html

Information on location of radioiodine treatment facilities in the UK:

University of Bristol Feline Centre.
www.langfordvets.co.uk/feline_medicine.htm

Animal Health Trust, Newmarket.
www.aht.org.uk/sa_medicine.html

Royal Veterinary College, London.
www.rvc.ac.uk/QMH/Specialities/InternalMedicine.cfm

Barton Veterinary Hospital, Canterbury.
www.barton-vets.co.uk

Rowe Vet Group, Wotton under Edge.
www.rowevetgroup.com/referral-services/iodine-radiation-therapy.aspx

University of Glasgow.
www.gla.ac.uk/schools/vet/smallanimalhospital/services/internalmedicine/

Bishopton Veterinary Group, North Yorkshire.
www.bishoptonvets.co.uk/small-and-domestic-animals.html

The University of Edinburgh Feline Clinic.
www.ed.ac.uk/schools-departments/vet/services/small-animals/referrals/services/thefelineclinic

Information on location of radioiodine treatment facilities in North America

A directory containing many of the treatment facilities in North America, according to their location can be found on
www.VeterinaryPartner.com/Content.plx?P=A&A=508&S=2&EVetID=0

Northwest Nuclear Medicine, Canada:
www.iodinecafe.com

Thyrocat treatment centres in Danbury, CT, Stamford CT, Long Island, NY, Auburn MA.
http://thyrocat.com/

Radiocat Clinics, in Phoenix, AZ; Los Angeles, CA; San Mateo, CA; Middletown, CT; New Castle, DE; Estero, FL; Marietta, GA; Arlington Heights, IL; Fishers, IN; Baltimore, MD; Wakefield, MA; Richmond, VA; Pittsburgh, PA; Greenville, SC and Springfield, VA.
www.radiocat.com/index.html

Information on location of radioiodine treatment facilities in Australia:

New South Wales
Double Bay Veterinary Clinic
www.doublebayvet.com.au/

Gladesville Veterinary Hospital
www.gladesvillevet.com.au/

University Veterinary Centre, Sydney
www.vetsci.usyd.edu.au/veterinary_services/sydney/referrals/medicine.shtml

Victoria

University of Melbourne

www.vch.unimelb.edu.au/group.php?groupID=524

Mt Evelyn Veterinary Clinic – no website. Telephone: 03 9736 3088

Seaford Veterinary Clinic – no website. Telephone: 03 9785 2611

Queensland

Chermside Veterinary Hospital – no website. Telephone: 07 3350 1333

South Australia

Adelaide Veterinary Specialist Centre

www.vetreferrals.com.au/Services/Feline-Radioactive-Iodine-Therapy.aspx

Australian Capital Territory

Canberra Veterinary Hospital

www.canberravet.com.au/Home.aspx

Information on location of radioiodine treatment facilities in New Zealand:

North Island

Auckland:

Veterinary Specialist Group

www.vsg.co.nz/

Lynfield Vet Clinic

www.lynfieldvet.co.nz/

Hamilton:

The Pet Practice

www.petpractice.co.nz/

Chartwell Vet Hospital – no website. Telephone: 07 855 9072

New Plymouth:

New Plymouth District Vet Group

www.npvet.co.nz/

Wellington:

Central Vet Hospital Ltd – Wellington

www.cenvet.co.nz/

Wadestown Vet Clinic – no website. Telephone: 04 472 2012

South Island

Christchurch:

McMaster and Heap Vet Practice

www.mcmasterheap.co.nz/mcmasterheap/

St Albans Vet Practice – no website. Telephone: 03 355 6747

The Straven Road Vet Centre

www.veterinarycentre.co.nz/index.php

Hornby Vet Centre

www.hornbyvet.co.nz/index.html

Rolleston Vet Services – no website. Telephone: 03 347 9682

Northlands Animal Care Hospital

www.northlandsanimalcare.co.nz/index.html

Telephone: 03 352 4335

Dunedin:

St Kilda Vet Centre – no website. Telephone: 03 455 2042

Please note, these may not be complete lists – your local vet should be able to tell you where the closest radioiodine facility is.

Glossary of terms used by vets

Term	Definition
Abscess	A pocket of infection, often containing a foul smelling purulent liquid (pus). One of the most common causes of an abscess is an infected wound resulting from a cat bite.
Acute kidney disease	Also referred to as acute renal failure (ARF). Sudden loss of kidney function which can be caused by one or more of the following: ■ Reduced blood supply to the kidneys (so called pre-renal AKD). Causes include heart failure and dehydration ■ Damage to the kidneys themselves (renal or intrinsic AKD). Causes include poisoning e.g. antifreeze (ethylene glycol), eating lilies ■ Failure of urine excretion due to urethral obstruction or rupture of the bladder. This is called post-renal AKD. Although many causes of AKD are fully treatable (and the kidney damage can be reversed), if severe and untreated, AKD can progress to permanent chronic kidney disease.
Anaesthesia	Providing a state of unconsciousness, muscle relaxation and loss of pain sensation using certain drugs (usually a combination of intravenously and by gas inhalation).
Anaemia	A reduction in the numbers of red blood cells in the circulation. Red blood cells (also known as erythrocytes) carry oxygen to the tissues of the body so anaemic cats will often be weak and listless. Anaemias are subdivided into: ■ Regenerative anaemias: ones in which the bone marrow (which manufactures red blood cells) is responding to the anaemia and trying to correct this ■ Non-regenerative anaemias: ones in which the bone marrow response (ability to produce more new erythrocytes) is insufficient or absent.
Apathetic (hyperthyroidism)	Cats showing depression, lethargy and reduced appetite are often referred to as 'apathetic' hyperthyroid cases. Some of these cats are even overweight rather than thin. Apathetic means that the cat appears indifferent, showing no emotion or animation. Most apathetic hyperthyroid cats are suffering from severe heart abnormalities associated with their hyperthyroidism.

Term	Definition
Antithyroid (medication)	Drug/s directed against the thyroid gland. Antithyroid medications (such as carbimazole and methimazole) block production of the thyroid hormones T3 and T4 by the thyroid gland.
Ascites	Accumulation of fluid in the abdominal cavity (the space around all of the abdominal organs).
Azotaemia	Accumulation of protein breakdown products such as urea and creatinine in the blood. Measurement of urea and creatinine levels is used to diagnose kidney disease and dehydration.
Biochemistry	Refers to blood tests of organ function (e.g. urea and creatinine), blood salt levels and protein levels.
Biopsy	Collection and laboratory analysis of a sample of tissue e.g. kidney biopsy.
Calcaemia	Referring to levels of calcium in the blood stream e.g. hypocalcaemia refers to sub-normal calcium levels.
Cancer	Illness caused by abnormal and uncontrolled growth of cells (sometimes referred to as persistent purposeless proliferation). Cancerous growths are malignant meaning that they not only grow where they originally start, but also can invade adjacent tissues and spread (metastasise) to other parts of the body. Common sites for metastasis include the lungs and liver. Left untreated, most cancers will ultimately cause the death of the cat.
Carcinoma	Malignant, cancerous growth of tissues such as the thyroid gland, skin or bowel.
Chronic kidney disease	Inadequate kidney function which has been present for at least 2 weeks. This is considered to be a progressive condition – it will get worse with time – although the speed of progression is variable.
Clinical examination	Examination of body systems by a veterinary surgeon or nurse. Typically this includes listening to the chest, opening the mouth and feeling the tummy.

Term	Definition
Clinical signs	The term used to describe what we would call our 'symptoms' if we were the cat e.g. sickness, loss of appetite.
Concurrent	Occurring at the same time.
Congenital	Congenital means present from birth.
Congestive heart failure	This describes the situation present when the heart is no longer able to pump effectively. Affected cats commonly suffer from breathing difficulties associated with pulmonary oedema or pleural effusion. Ascites can also be seen in cats with congestive heart failure.
Cystitis	Inflammation of the urinary bladder (where urine is stored before urination). One cause would be a bacterial infection of the urine.
Cystocentesis	Technique of urine collection using a needle and syringe. The needle is passed through the skin and into the bladder from which urine is collected.
Diabetes mellitus	Also referred to as 'sugar diabetes'. Cats with this condition are unable to regulate their blood sugar levels due to a lack of insulin (a hormone that helps control blood glucose levels) or insulin resistance (interference with the way that insulin works). Insulin is produced by the pancreas and facilitates absorption of glucose into the cells of the body. Affected cats have high blood sugar levels and common clinical signs are an increased thirst, increased amount of urine produced and weight loss in spite of a good or even increased appetite. Treatment of diabetes usually involves changes to the diet and, in many cases, injections of insulin. Hyperthyroidism can cause insulin resistance and it is not unusual to see both illnesses in the same cat.
Ectopic	Occurring in an abnormal or unusual location. For example ectopic thyroid tissue can be present under the base of the tongue or in the chest cavity.
Erythrocyte	Red blood cell. These are the cells that carry oxygen in the circulation. A lack of red blood cells is called anaemia.

Term	Definition
Erythrocytosis	This term describes the situation when there are increased numbers of red blood cells present in the circulation. Causes include dehydration, certain medical disorders (including hyperthyroidism) and bone marrow disorders.
Euthanased	The process of euthanasia (see below).
Euthanasia	Also referred to as 'putting to sleep' this is the term used when a veterinarian ends a cat's life. This is usually done by giving an overdose of barbiturate anaesthetic into a vein – the cat dies within seconds of the injection being given.
Euthyroid, euthyroidism	Having normal blood levels of thyroid hormones. Presence of other illnesses (such as chronic kidney disease) can reduce the blood levels of total T4 and in some cats this can reduce the T4 levels into the reference range (i.e. giving a falsely normal result). This phenomenon is known as 'sick euthyroid' and defines the situation where other illnesses suppress the levels of thyroid hormones.
Goitre	An enlarged thyroid gland which can be felt through the skin. In some cases, the goitre is so large that it can be seen.
Haematology	Laboratory test assessing the blood count, numbers and types of white blood cells and platelets.
History	This is the process by which your veterinarian gathers information on your cat and all of its problems (clinical signs).
Hyper-	Increased e.g. hyperkalaemia, hypercalcaemia: increased blood potassium levels, increased blood calcium levels.
Hyperthyroidism	Also referred to as thyrotoxicosis. This is the veterinary term used to describe an illness resulting from having excessively high blood levels of thyroid hormones. The thyroid hormones are required in healthy cats for many functions including normal growth and development. Excessive blood levels of thyroid hormones (such as is the case with hyperthyroidism) are damaging to the body and ultimately this is a fatal illness if not treated.

Term	Definition
Hypo-	Reduced e.g. hypokalaemia: low levels of potassium in the blood; hypotension: low blood pressure.
Hypocalcaemia	Low blood calcium levels. Hypocalcaemia is potential complication associated with thyroid surgery and it can be associated with very severe, even fatal consequences.
Hypoparathyroidism	Under-functioning of the parathyroid gland which causes reduced production of parathyroid hormones. Parathyroid hormones are needed for normal control of blood calcium levels. Hypoparathyroidism is a potential complication of thyroid surgery and can cause severe hypocalcaemia.
Hypothyroidism	Under-functioning of the thyroid gland which causes reduced production of thyroid hormones. Thyroid hormones are needed for normal control of metabolic processes in the body. Hypothyroidism can occur as a congenital disease but is most common following treatment for hyperthyroidism.
Inflammation	A response of injured or damaged cells which helps to wall off the problem, eliminate infectious substances (for example) and restore healthy tissue. The classic signs of inflammation are: ■ Heat ■ Pain ■ Redness ■ Swelling ■ Loss of function.
Inflammatory	Pertaining to inflammation.
Kidney disease	See acute and chronic kidney disease.

Term	Definition
Laryngeal paralysis	An inability to fully open the larynx (voice box) when breathing, caused by damage to the recurrent laryngeal nerve. Laryngeal paralysis is a rare complication of hyperthyroidism and can also be caused by thyroid surgery. Affected cats can suffer from an altered voice, breathing difficulties, noisy breathing and a cough. In severe cases, surgery may be required to treat the laryngeal paralysis. This is a very rare potential complication of thyroid surgery.
Oedema	The accumulation of excessive amounts of watery fluid in the cells or spaces between the cells.
Parathyroid	These small glands are located very close to the thyroid tissue and help to control blood levels of calcium. Two pairs of parathyroid gland are present in each cat – one pair lying outside the thyroid gland and the other pair lying inside the capsule that surrounds the thyroid. If these delicate structures are damaged or removed during thyroid surgery, affected cats can suffer from hypocalcaemia (low blood calcium levels) which can be fatal if not treated. This condition is called hypoparathyroidism.
Pathologist	A specialist in pathology who is able to diagnose the cause and/or type of disease by examining biopsy samples.
Pathology	The study of disease.
Pleural effusion	Accumulation of fluid in the chest space around the lungs.
Polydipsia	An increased thirst.
Polyphagia	An increased appetite.
Polyuria	Increased volume of urine produced (usually noticed as the cat is passing normal volumes of urine more frequently).
Prognosis	A forecast of the likely long-term outlook for a cat with a given condition/s.

Term	Definition
Pulmonary oedema	The accumulation of excessive amounts of watery fluid in the cells or spaces between the cells of the lungs. This is a common consequence of congestive heart failure in cats. Affected cats often suffer from breathlessness and are very lethargic.
Radiograph/s	X-ray/s.
Radioiodine	A form of radiotherapy that is able to treat abnormal thyroid tissue. Radioiodine contains a very small dose of radioactive iodine (131I) which is given orally or by injection. Iodine is used by the thyroid gland to produce thyroid hormones. The radioactivity is able to destroy the abnormal thyroid tissue, shrinking the goitre and reducing the amount of thyroid hormones produced.
Recurrent laryngeal nerve	This is one of the nerves that supplies the larynx (voice box). Temporary or permanent damage can occur during surgery and is called laryngeal paralysis (paralysis of the larynx).
Refractometer/s	Instrument/s that can measure the concentration of urine.
Scintigraphy	This technique is also referred to as a technetium scan, isotope scan or radionuclide imaging. It describes the use of radioactive substances to make an image of tissues. Thyroid scintigraphy can be used to locate abnormal thyroid tissue and is particularly helpful in cats with ectopic thyroid disease.
Sedation	Providing a state of calm and muscle relaxation using drugs. The cat is still conscious but, depending on the drugs used, may appear quite sleepy.
Stricture/s	The medical term for an abnormal narrowing of a tube such as the oesophagus (food pipe). Causes of strictures include tumours and inflammation.
Sympathetic nervous system	Nerves involved in this part of the nervous system pass close to the thyroid glands and can be damaged during surgery. Affected cats can develop temporary or permanent Horner's syndrome. This is recognised as a droopy upper eyelid, smaller pupil, a sunken eye (ptosis) and protrusion of the third eyelid (sometimes referred to as the Haws or nictitating membrane). This is a very rare potential complication of thyroid surgery and is usually temporary although it may take weeks or months to resolve.

Term	Definition
Systemic hypertension	An increase in the blood pressure of the systemic blood supply (the blood supply to all of the body except the lungs).
T3	One of the thyroid hormones. Its full name is triiodothyronine.
T4	One of the thyroid hormones. Its full name is thyroxine.
Thyroid	The thyroid gland is normally located in the cat's neck, just below the larynx (voice box). The thyroid gland is made up of two lobes – one on each side of the body. The thyroid gland produces thyroid hormones (T3 and T4) which are needed to regulate metabolic processes in the body.
Thyroidectomy	Surgical removal of all or part of the thyroid gland.
Transdermal	Transdermal medications come as a skin cream which is usually applied to the inside of the cat's ear (a hairless area). The medication is absorbed through the skin and into the blood stream. Transdermal antithyroid medications can take longer to be effective than the oral form. Transdermal medications are controversial – there is much less evidence to demonstrate their effectiveness. The skin normally forms a barrier to stop substances from entering the body so this might not always be a good way of delivering a drug to the blood stream.
Trauma	Injury or wound.
Urethra	The tube which carries urine from the bladder to the outside of the body.
Urethral obstruction	This is the medical term for a 'blocked cat'. A blockage in the urethra prevents the cat from being able to pass urine. This is an emergency condition since it can be fatal if left untreated.
Urinalysis	Laboratory analysis of a urine sample e.g. concentration, number of cells, acidity, protein levels.

Converting SI units to Conventional units and vice versa

Parameter	To convert Conventional to SI multiply by...	To convert SI to Conventional multiply by...
Albumin	10	0.1
Alanine aminotransferase (ALT)	1	1
Alkaline phosphatase (ALP)	1	1
Bicarbonate	1	1
Calcium	0.25	4
Cholesterol	0.0259	38.61
Creatinine	88.4	0.0113
Free T4 (fT4)	12.9	0.0775
Glucose	0.0555	18.02
Haemoglobin (Hb)	10	0.1
Packed cell volume (PCV) or haematocrit	0.01	100
Phosphate	0.323	3.1
Potassium	1	1
Sodium	1	1
Total protein	10	0.1
Total Thyroxine (tT4)	12.9	0.0775
Urea	0.357	2.8